2021 Home Builders' Jobsite Codes:
A Quick Guide to the 2021 International Residential Code

NAHB.
National Association
of Home Builders

ICC
INTERNATIONAL
CODE COUNCIL

2021 Home Builders' Jobsite Codes:
A Quick Guide to the 2021 International Residential Code

BuilderBooks, a Service of the National Association of Home Builders

Patricia Potts	Senior Director
Circle Graphics	Cover Design
Robert Brown Jr.	Composition
Gerald M. Howard	NAHB Chief Executive Officer
Mark A. Johnson	ICC Executive Vice President, Business Development
Hamid Naderi, P.E., CBO	ICC Senior Vice President, Product Development
Doug Thornburg, AIA, CBO	ICC Vice President and
	Technical Director Products and Services
Steve Van Note, CBO	Author

Disclaimer

This publication is provided for information purposes only. It is not intended to serve as a substitute for the *2021 International Residential Code*, as a basis for complying with it, or as an alternative to any state or local building code or ordinance. It is not offered for the purpose of providing professional advice, either from a legal, accounting, or other professional service standpoint. It is recommended that you consult with an experienced professional in the interpretation and/or application of the information so provided. Reference herein to any specific commercial products, process, or service by trade name, trademark, manufacturer, or otherwise does not necessarily constitute or imply its endorsement, recommendation, or favored status by the National Association of Home Builders. The views and opinions of the author expressed in this publication do not necessarily state or reflect those of the National Association of Home Builders, and they shall not be used to advertise or endorse a product.

Printed in the United States of America

26 25 24   2 3 4 5

ISBN-13: 978-0-86718-787-8
eISBN-13: 978-0-86718-788-5

For further information, please contact:

National Association of Home Builders	International Code Council®
1201 15th Street, NW	500 New Jersey Avenue, NW, 6th Floor
Washington, DC 20005-2800	Washington, DC 20001-2070
BuilderBooks.com	888-ICC-SAFE (422-7233)
	iccsafe.org

About The Author

Steve Van Note has over 45 years of experience in the construction and building code arena. He spent 14 years with the product development team for the International Code Council (ICC), where he developed technical resource materials in support of the International Codes. His role also included the management, review, and technical editing of publications developed by ICC staff members and other expert authors. He has authored a number of ICC support publications including *Significant Changes to the International Residential Code, Residential Code Essentials* and *Inspector Skills*. In addition, Steve developed and presented *International Residential Code* seminars nationally. Prior to joining ICC in 2006, Steve was a building official for Linn County, Iowa. Prior to his 15 years at Linn County, he was a carpenter and construction project manager for residential, commercial, and industrial buildings.

Contents

Figures

Chapter 2. Fire Safety

Chapter 15. Electrical Systems

Tables

Chapter 5. Floors

Chapter 6. Wall Construction

Chapter 8. Roof Framing

Chapter 15. Electrical Systems

Acknowledgments

The author is grateful to Ron Van Note, master carpenter and builder, for his usual expert counsel.

Introduction

Home Builders' Jobsite Codes is a field guide for builders, trade contractors, design professionals, inspectors, and others involved in the design and construction of residential buildings. It is based on the *2021 International Residential Code*® (IRC). This comprehensive stand-alone code establishes minimum regulations for the construction of one- and two-family *dwellings and townhomes*. It includes provisions for

- Structural design
- Fire and life safety
- Energy conservation
- Mechanical systems
- Fuel-gas systems
- Plumbing
- Electrical systems

The IRC's purpose is to safeguard public safety, health, and general welfare from fire and other potential hazards attributed to the built environment, while keeping homes affordable. The code provides for strong, stable, and sanitary homes that conserve energy and yet offer adequate lighting and ventilation.

Published by the International Code Council® (ICC), the IRC is maintained and updated through an open code development process and is available internationally for adoption by governing authorities.

Home Builders' Jobsite Codes focuses on the prescriptive provisions of the IRC—"recipes," if you will, for meeting code requirements without the need for an engineered design. These provisions address all aspects of conventional construction of dwellings and their accessory buildings. Illustrations and tables assist the reader in understanding the code requirements and address frequently asked questions. Some terms appear in italics the first time they are used in the text. The glossary at the back of the book defines these terms. *Home Builders' Jobsite Codes* also includes other useful information not in the IRC, such as weights of building materials and components.

Although this guide is organized into chapters similar to the IRC, there are some important exceptions. For example, for ease of use, IRC "Building Planning" requirements, detailed in chapter 3 of the code itself, are divided into three separate chapters in this pocket guide:
1. Structural Design Criteria
2. Fire Safety
3. Safe and Healthy Living Environments

Home Builders' Jobsite Codes explores these important issues in more detail in other chapters as well.

Home Builders' Jobsite Codes is not an official code, and has not been adopted as such in any jurisdiction. The publication intends to serve as a guide only. It does not include all applicable requirements of the IRC. For example, certain *performance* criteria related to engineered design are outside the limited scope of this publication. Builders should consult the IRC, local amendments, and local building departments for more detailed requirements and for criteria related to other methods of construction.

Builders also should obtain specific information on design criteria for wind, snow, seismic (earthquake) events, flood, soil, or other atmospheric and geological conditions, as well as any amendments to the code, from their local building departments.

Since code requirements for energy conservation, decay resistance, and termite control requirements also may vary by geographic region, builders should obtain that information from local building code departments.

For more information on the *2021 International Residential Code,* go online to the International Code Council's Web site, www.iccsafe.org, or call 1-888-ICC-SAFE (422-7233).

1

Structural Design Criteria

The IRC establishes minimum structural design criteria necessary to accommodate normal loads placed on a building and, depending on a home's location, resist the forces of natural hazards such as snow, wind, earthquake, and flood. In most cases, the tried-and-true construction practices offered in the IRC incorporate these criteria, eliminating the need for an engineered design or complex calculations. For example, the code provides span tables for conventional wood framing elements such as joists, girders, headers, and rafters.

Construction must safely support all loads:

- Snow, wind, seismic, and flood loads, which vary by geographic region
- *Live loads*
- *Dead loads*
- *Roof loads*

Note: The roof is designed for the roof live load (not more than 20 psf) or the snow load, whichever is greater.

To correctly apply the values of the tables and the prescriptive methods of construction, builders must know the structural design criteria in the planning chapter of the code. Determining the appropriate live loads is fairly straightforward. However, seismic, wind, snow, soil, or flood area values differ by geographic location. In addition, frost depth, weathering severity, ice barrier underlayment requirements, and history of termite damage vary by climate and geography. Therefore, builders often must obtain information through the maps found in the IRC or through their local building departments.

Moreover, some structural elements still may require an engineered design. For example, the sizing of wide-flange steel beams commonly used in dwelling construction is outside the scope of the IRC. Instead, accepted engineering practices will determine their sizes.

Live Loads

Minimum required live loads for floors are based on the use of the space. Guards and handrails also must be secured to safely resist forces against them (table 1.1).

Table 1.1 Minimum uniformly distributed live loads

Use	Uniform load (psf)	Concentrated load (lb)
Uninhabitable attics without storage	10	
Uninhabitable attics with limited storage	20	
Habitable attics and attics served with fixed stairs	30	
Decks and exterior balconies	40	
Guards		200
Guard in-fill		50
Handrail		200
Passenger vehicle garages	50	2,000
Areas other than sleeping areas	40	
Sleeping areas	30	
Stairs	40	300

Deflection

Allowable deflection is a measurement of bending under code-prescribed loads to ensure adequate stiffness of structural framing members such as studs, joists, beams, and rafters (table 1.2). Although the prescriptive tables account for deflection in their values, builders must be familiar with deflection limits in order to choose the appropriate table for sizing a framing member. Allowable deflection is measured by dividing the span or length (L) of the member by a prescribed factor, such as 360 for floor joists (L/360). To determine allowable deflection for a certain span, convert feet to inches and divide the result by 360. The following example is for a floor joist with a 16 ft. span:

L = 16 ft. × 12 in. = 192 in.

Allowable deflection = 192 in. / 360 = 0.53 in.

Allowable deflection for this floor joist is approximately ½ in.

Note: A 16 ft. span rafter with a ⁴⁄12 slope and no ceiling attached has an allowable deflection of L/180, which is twice the deflection allowed for floor joists.

Table 1.2 Allowable deflection of structural members

Structural member	Allowable deflection
Rafters, slope > ³⁄₁₂, no finished ceiling attached to rafters	L/180
Rafters, slope > ³⁄₁₂, finished ceiling attached to rafters	L/240
Ceiling joist	L/240
Plastered ceilings	L/360
Floors	L/360
All other structural members	L/240

Note: Wall deflection and wind load deflections are not shown.

Calculating Dead Loads

The prescriptive tables of the IRC detailing continuous footing sizes for conventional frame construction assume average weights of construction materials. Therefore, additional calculations typically are not required. The material and component weights (tables 1.3 and 1.4) may help builders correctly size an isolated footing, or another element not covered in the IRC tables.

Table 1.3 Building material weights

Materials	Weight (psf)
Plywood – ¼ in.	.8
Plywood – ½ in.	1.6
Plywood – ¾ in.	2.4
4" Brick	35.0
Gypsum board – ½ in.	2.1
Gypsum board – ⅝ in.	2.5
Quarry tile – ½ in.	5.8
Hardwood flooring – ²⁵⁄₃₂ in.	4.0
Built-up roofing	6.5
Shingles, asphalt	1.7–2.8
Shingles, wood	2.0–3.0
Common dimension lumber (lb. per cu. ft.)	27–29 lb. per cu. ft.
Concrete (lb. per cu. yd.)	150 lb. per cu. ft.

Table 1.4 Average weights of building components

Description	Weight (psf)
Roof dead load (framing, sheathing, asphalt shingles, insulation, drywall)	10
Exterior wall (2 × 4 framing, sheathing, siding, insulation, drywall)	10
Floor (joist, sheathing, carpeting, drywall)	10
Concrete wall–8 in. thick	100
10 in. thick	125
12 in. thick	150
Concrete block wall–8 in. thick	60

Wind

The prescriptive structural provisions of the IRC are limited to those geographical regions with wind speeds of 140 mph or less (130 mph in hurricane-prone regions) as defined in the IRC wind maps. Otherwise, the code requires a design in accordance with one of the referenced standards. In addition to an engineered design that complies with the *International Building Code* (IBC)[1] and ASCE 7,[2] the IRC includes references to ICC 600, *Standard for Residential Construction in High Wind Regions*[3] and *AWC Wood Frame Construction Manual* (WFCM).[4]

Wind Exposure Category

In addition to the basic wind speeds for a geographic area, ground surface irregularities affect the wind's impact on a building. The IRC classifies wind exposure into three categories:

1. Exposure B—some wind protection with trees and buildings characteristic of urban and suburban settings
2. Exposure C—open terrain with scattered obstructions
3. Exposure D—adjacent to large bodies of water, including hurricane-prone regions

Exposure categories are important design criteria for engineering purposes. For many of the prescriptive methods of wood frame construction in the IRC, wind exposure category is not a factor. However, wind exposure category must be considered when applying the provisions for wall sheathing, wood wall bracing, roof tie-down, and exterior wall and roof coverings. The following components must be *designed* and installed to resist wind loads based on the wind speed and exposure category:

- Siding
- Roof covering
- Windows

- Skylights
- Exterior doors
- Overhead doors

Hurricanes

Hurricane-prone regions are the coastal areas of the Atlantic Ocean and Gulf of Mexico where the ultimate design wind speed is greater than 115 mph. The IRC wind maps identify the portions of hurricane-prone regions that require an engineered design or a design that complies with other referenced standards. Windows and other glazing require additional protection if they are in *windborne debris regions*—those areas within hurricane-prone regions as specifically defined in the code.

Storm Shelters

Storm shelters, sometimes called *safe rooms,* are not required by the code. However, they offer added protection from the destructive forces of high winds, hurricanes, and tornadoes. When installed within a dwelling or as a separate structure, storm shelters must conform to the requirements of ICC-500, *Standard on the Design and Construction of Storm Shelters.*[5]

Earthquake

The IRC assigns a *seismic design category* (SDC) to building sites relative to the anticipated intensity and frequency of earthquakes. (For more details, see the seismic map in the code.) For buildings located in SDC A or B and constructed under the prescriptive methods of the IRC, there are no additional seismic requirements. One- and two-family dwellings in SDC C also are exempt from the seismic requirements. However, specific seismic requirements apply to townhomes sited in SDC C, and to all buildings in SDC D_0, D_1, and D_2.

The higher seismic design categories (SDC D_0, D_1, and D_2) occur predominantly in western parts of the U.S., in the New Madrid area of Missouri, Illinois, Indiana, Tennessee, and Arkansas, and in South Carolina.

2

Fire Safety

Fire-resistant construction is required to separate
dwelling units, for exterior walls located close to
property lines, and on the garage side of an attached
garage/dwelling separation.

This chapter addresses these requirements, as
well as protection of floor assemblies and foam plastic
insulation, fire sprinkler systems, smoke alarms, and
emergency escape. Fire protection related to specific
building components is addressed throughout the
code and is detailed in this and other chapters of this
book.

Location on Property

Exterior walls of dwellings and garages must maintain a minimum separation from the property line,
measured perpendicular to the wall, or be protected
for fire. For dwellings without fire sprinkler systems,
walls less than 5 ft. from the property line must have

a fire-resistance rating of one hour when exposed to fire from either side of the wall. The code permits a 3 ft. separation without a fire-resistance-rated wall when the dwelling has an automatic fire sprinkler system. A typical one-hour wall assembly consists of ⅝ in. Type X gypsum board or gypsum sheathing on both sides of a frame wall with insulation filling the cavity. However, a number of other approved designs are available.

The following fire-resistance requirements are based on distances to the property line (figs. 2.1 and 2.2):

For dwellings without fire sprinklers:

- Less than 5 ft.—one-hour wall
- Less than 5 ft.—limited area for windows and doors
- Less than 3 ft.—no windows or doors
- Less than 2 ft.—no roof overhang projections

Roof overhang projections less than 5 ft. from the property line require one-hour protection on their underside.

For dwellings with fire sprinklers:

- Less than 3 ft.—one-hour wall
- Less than 3 ft.—no windows or doors
- Less than 2 ft.—no roof overhang projections

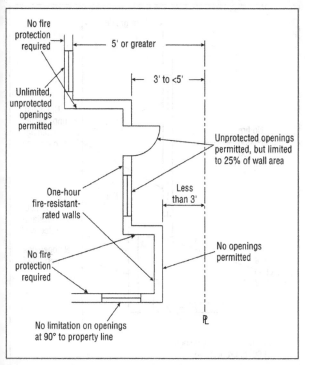

Figure 2.1 Exterior wall location near lot line for dwellings without fire sprinklers

Figure 2.2 Exterior wall location near lot line for dwellings with fire sprinklers

Roof overhang projections less than 3 ft. from the property line require one-hour protection on their undersides.

Note: Sheds and playhouses of 200 sq. ft. or less do not require fire-resistant protection regardless of their location on the property.

Dwelling Unit Separation

Fire-resistant-rated separations are required between dwelling units of duplexes and townhomes as follows:

Two-Family Dwelling Separation

- One-hour fire-resistance-rated construction is required to completely separate dwelling units.
- The separating wall assemblies must extend from the foundation to the underside of the roof sheathing and to the exterior walls (fig. 2.3).
  There is one exception:
  - Wall assemblies need not extend through the attic if ⅝ in. Type X gypsum board is installed on the ceiling of the living space and an attic draft stop lines up with the separating wall.

Note: The fire resistance requirements for duplexes are the same whether there is a lot line or no lot line between the dwelling units. (fig. 2.4)

Figure 2.3 Fire-resistant-rated separation between dwelling units of duplex

Figure 2.4 Duplex dwelling units separated by lot line and 1-hr. fire-resistant wall

Townhome Separation

Townhome dwelling units require separation with two 1-hour fire-resistance-rated wall assemblies or a common wall. The fire-resistance rating of the common wall separating townhome dwelling units depends on the presence or absence of an automatic fire sprinkler system. Townhomes without sprinkler protection require a 2-hr. rated separation whereas the rating is reduced to 1 hr. for townhomes with sprinkler systems (fig. 2.5). Additional requirements follow:

- The common separation wall cannot contain plumbing, mechanical equipment, vents, or ducts.
- The separation wall must be continuous from the foundation to the underside of the roof sheathing.
- Parapets are not required when certain fire-resistant protection is provided for the roof for 4 ft. on both sides of the separating wall.
- Common walls must extend to the exterior sheathing of the exterior walls.

Note: The common wall is permitted to terminate at the interior side of the exterior wall where a double stud is installed as fireblocking in the exterior wall.

Plumbing vent

Fire-retardant wood (FRT) sheathing (or non-combustible sheathing or 5/8 in. type X gypsum board below sheathing)

Gas vent

No roof openings within 4' of separating wall

4' min.   4' min.

Roof trusses

Townhome Unit A

Townhome Unit B

No plumbing, ducts or vents in common wall

Common fire-resistant-rated wall: 1-hr for townhomes with sprinkler systems; 2-hr for townhomes without sprinklers

Common foundation

Figure 2.5 Fire-resistant-rated common wall between townhomes

Fire-Resistant-Rated Penetrations

When items such as pipes or ducts penetrate one or both sides of the fire-resistant-rated wall or the floor/ceiling assemblies separating dwelling units, both the penetrating item and the space around it must be protected to maintain fire resistance. In general, penetrations by steel, ferrous and copper pipe, tubing, and conduit require only that the space left around the pipe be filled with approved materials to limit the passage of fire. The material, such as a *listed* fire caulk, must be installed according to the manufacturer's instructions to provide a fire-resistant time rating equivalent to that of the construction being penetrated.

Other penetrating materials, such as plastic plumbing pipe, (not permitted for the common wall separating townhome dwelling units), must be protected further by approved means, such as a listed firestop assembly, to maintain the fire-resistance rating of the wall or floor/ceiling assembly. Steel electrical boxes up to 16 sq. in. and listed electrical boxes of any material are permitted if they are separated by approved means when they are located on opposite sides of the wall. Wood blocking or applying listed putty pads to both boxes are two means of separating them.

Garages

Attached garages and detached garages within 3 ft. of
the residence require protection to resist the spread
of fire to the dwelling, but not the same protection as
required between dwelling units (fig. 2.6). The separation does not require an assembly with a fire-resistance
rating as in the case of dwelling unit separations. The
prescriptive requirements are as follows:

- To provide separation of the garage from the dwelling, ½ in. gypsum board must be installed on the
  garage side.
- If habitable rooms are located above the garage,
  ⅝ in. Type X gypsum board must be installed on
  the garage ceiling and ½ in. gypsum board must be
  installed on the walls supporting the floor/ceiling.
- Doors between the dwelling and garage must be
  self-closing and self-latching, and one of the following types:
  - 1⅜ in.-thick solid wood
  - 1⅜ in.-thick solid-core steel
  - 1⅜ in.-thick honeycomb-core steel
  - 20-minute fire rated
- Ducts in the garage as well as ducts penetrating the
  walls or ceilings that separate the dwelling from the
  garage shall be of a minimum No. 26 gage sheet steel.
  The ducts shall have no openings into the garage.

Figure 2.6 Garage separation from dwelling (habitable space above garage)

- Garages cannot open into a sleeping room.
- Garage floors shall be noncombustible and sloped to a drain or the vehicle entry door.

Fire Protection of Floors

For certain types of floor framing such as open-web trusses and I-joists, the IRC requires application of a membrane to the underside of the framing to provide limited fire protection and delay collapse of the floor in a fire. The membrane must be one of the following materials:

- ½ in. gypsum wallboard
- ⅝ in. wood structural panel
- Other equivalent material

Protection is not required for floor assemblies:

- Over a space protected with automatic fire sprinklers
- Over a crawl space not intended for storage or heating appliances
- With unprotected portions not greater than 80 sq. ft. per story isolated by prescribed fireblocking
- Of 2 × 10 or greater dimension lumber or structural composite lumber

Foam Plastic Insulation

A thermal barrier of ½ in. gypsum board or equivalent must separate foam plastic from the interior. The following exceptions are permitted:

- In attics and crawl spaces entered only for repairs or maintenance, foam plastic may be covered with one of the following ignition-barrier materials:
  - 1½ in. mineral fiber insulation
  - ¼ in. *wood structural panels*
  - ⅜ in. particleboard

- ¼ in. hardboard
- ⅜ in. gypsum board
- 0.016 in. corrosion-resistant steel
- 1½-inch-thick cellulose insulation
- ¼-inch fiber-cement panel, soffit or backer board

■ Foam plastic may be spray applied to a sill plate and header (rim joist area) without the thermal barrier when the foam plastic meets the following requirements:

- No more than 3¼ in. thick
- Density of 1½–2 lb. per cu. ft.
- Flame-spread index less than or equal to 25 and smoke-developed index less than or equal to 450

Other types of insulation and insulation facings or vapor barriers also may require covering with ½ in. gypsum board or other approved materials, depending on flame-spread and smoke-developed properties of the exposed material.

Automatic Fire Sprinkler Systems

A dwelling unit fire sprinkler system helps to detect and control fires and is meant to prevent *flashover* in the room where a fire originates to allow time for occupants to escape a building. The code requires an automatic fire sprinkler system in new townhomes and new one- and two-family dwellings.

The sprinkler system must conform to one of the following:

- IRC sec. P2904, Dwelling Unit Fire Sprinkler Systems

or

- NFPA 13D, *Standard for the Installation of Sprinkler Systems in One- and Two-Family Dwellings and Manufactured Homes*

A dwelling unit fire sprinkler system requires less water compared with NFPA 13 and 13R systems. It may be either a multipurpose or stand-alone system. The code permits connection to many types of water supply systems to meet the required fire sprinkler system capacity. Generally, a dwelling unit fire sprinkler system does not require sprinklers in the following locations:

- Closets not greater than 24 sq. ft. with a depth of 3 ft. or less
- *Bathrooms* no larger than 55 sq. ft.
- Open porches
- Garages
- Attics without a fuel-fired appliance
- Crawl spaces
- Concealed spaces

Dwelling fire sprinkler systems also do not require a fire department connection.

Note: The IRC requires a single sprinkler above fuel-fired equipment installed in an attic.

Smoke Alarms

Dwelling units require smoke alarms as follows:

Required Locations

In new homes and dwelling units undergoing remodeling, the code requires a smoke alarm in the following locations:

- Each sleeping room
- Outside of and in the immediate vicinity of each separate sleeping area
- On each story, including basements and *habitable attics*

Note: Where the ceiling of a room is greater than 24 inches higher than an adjoining hallway that serves a bedroom, both locations require a smoke alarm.

Required Clearances

To prevent nuisance alarms, the code requires the following minimum clearances for smoke alarms:

- 3 ft. horizontally from a bathroom door
- 20 ft. horizontally from a cooking appliance for ionization smoke alarms

- 10 ft. horizontally from a cooking appliance for ionization smoke alarms with an alarm-silencing switch
- 6 ft. horizontally from a cooking appliance for photoelectric smoke alarms and other alarms marked for such location

Installation Requirements

The smoke alarms must meet the following installation requirements:

- Hardwired to the building power with no disconnection switch
- Battery backup
- Alarms interconnected

Note: The code allows listed wireless alarms in place of physical interconnection. All alarms must sound upon activation of one alarm.

Additions, Alterations, and Repairs

For construction that requires a permit, other than deck and porch additions and exterior work, such as siding, windows, doors, and roofing, dwelling units must have smoke alarms located as required for new construction.

Smoke alarms may be battery operated without connection to the building wiring. The code requires interconnection of alarms, which may be accomplished with wireless alarms.

Emergency Escape and Rescue Openings

One of the most important safety provisions in the IRC is for emergency escape and rescue openings. These openings provide a secondary means to exit a sleeping room or basement if a fire blocks the usual means of egress. They must allow occupants to escape directly to a yard or open space and allow rescue personnel fully equipped with breathing apparatus to enter the room from the outside. Typically these openings are windows or doors; however, other openings may be approved.

Required Locations

Occupants are most vulnerable to the hazards of fire when they are not fully alert or when they are in spaces that have no windows or doors. The code addresses these life-safety issues by requiring an emergency escape and rescue opening in the following locations:

- Every sleeping room
- Habitable attics
- Basements, unless they are not more than 200 sq. ft. and are used only for mechanical equipment or a storm shelter

Note: For other than new sleeping rooms, the code does not require installation of an emergency escape and rescue opening in an existing basement undergoing remodeling or repairs.

Note: *Sleeping rooms in basements do not require emergency escape and rescue openings when the dwelling is protected with a fire sprinkler system and the basement has an emergency escape and rescue opening in addition to the usual means of egress.*

General Requirements
In an emergency, occupants need to move quickly and easily to the safety of the outdoors. Therefore, emergency escape and rescue openings must
- Open to a public way, yard, or court
- Open from the inside without the use of keys, tools, or special knowledge

Dimensions
In order for emergency escape and rescue openings to serve their intended purpose, the code limits the sill height above the floor and prescribes minimum dimensions as follows (table 2.1 and fig. 2.7):
- 5.7 sq. ft. net opening (5 sq. ft. for grade floor opening)
- 24 in. minimum net opening height
- 20 in. minimum net opening width
- 44 in. maximum sill height
- 36-in.-high by 36-in.-wide path to yard or court when the emergency escape window is under a deck or porch

Table 2.1 Minimum net clear width/height combinations for 5.7 sq. ft. emergency escape and rescue openings (in.)

Width	20	20.5	21	21.5	22	22.5
Height	41	40	39.1	38.2	37.3	36.5
Width	23	23.5	24	24.5	25	25.5
Height	35.7	34.9	34.2	33.5	32.8	32.2
Width	26	26.5	27	27.5	28	28.5
Height	31.6	31	30.4	29.8	29.3	28.8
Width	29	29.5	30	30.5	31	31.5
Height	28.3	27.8	27.4	26.9	26.5	26.1
Width	32	32.5	33	33.5	34	34.2
Height	25.7	25.3	24.9	24.5	24.1	24

Figure 2.7 Emergency escape and rescue windows

Window Well

The code requires a window well if the sill of the
emergency escape opening is below grade (fig. 2.8).
Window wells shall

- Be at least 9 sq. ft. in area
- Have a minimum dimension of 36 in.
- Allow the emergency escape element to fully open

If a window well is more than 44 in. deep, it must
have a ladder or steps. Ladders and steps may
encroach 6 in. into the required space. Ladders must
meet the following requirements:

- Be at least 12 in. wide
- Project at least 3 in.
- Have rungs spaced not more than 18 in.

Stairs must meet the following requirements:

- Be at least 12 in. wide
- Have treads at least 5 in. deep
- Have risers not more than 18 in. high

Approved bars, grilles, or covers are permitted over
emergency escape windows or window wells
if they

- Maintain net opening dimensions
- Can be released or removed from the inside without the use of a key, tool, special knowledge, or

force greater than that required for normal operation of the escape and rescue opening

Window wells serving emergency escape openings must have provisions for drainage to the foundation drain.

Figure 2.8 Window well for emergency escape and rescue opening

3

Safe and Healthy Living Environments

Although structural integrity and fire protection were addressed generally in the previous chapters, this chapter includes other minimum requirements for constructing safe and healthy living environments, including *means of egress,* carbon monoxide alarms, room dimensions, ventilation, protection from decay, and safety glazing.

Means of Egress

Stairways, ramps, hallways, and doors are the primary means of egress from dwelling units. The means of egress provides a continuous unobstructed path from all portions of the dwelling to the outdoors through the required exit door without passing through the garage. There must be at least one exterior exit door meeting the minimum size requirements. Otherwise, the code does not specify minimum door sizes. Hallways must be at least 3 ft. wide. To provide fire protection for the egress path, enclosed accessible space under stairs must be protected on the enclosed side with ½ in. gypsum board.

Doors

All dwelling units require at least one exterior exit door (typically a 3 ft. by 6 ft. 8 in. standard door) that meets the following criteria:

- Side hinged
- At least 32 in. wide net opening
- At least 78 in. high net opening
- Readily openable from the inside without the use of a key or special knowledge or effort

Landings for Doors

Generally, each exterior door must have a landing on the exterior side that is at least as wide as the door and 36 in. in the direction of travel (fig. 3.1). At the required exit door, the maximum threshold height is

- 1½ in. above the interior floor
- 7¾ in. above the exterior landing when the door swings in
- 1½ in. above the exterior landing when the door swings out

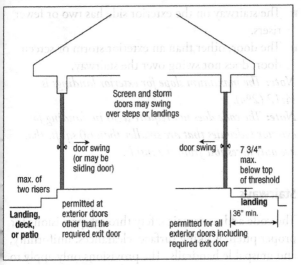

Figure 3.1 Landings at exterior doors

For exterior doors other than the required exit door, the maximum threshold height is

- 7¾ in. above the interior floor
- 7¾ in. above the exterior landing

The exterior side of a door does not require a landing under the following conditions:

- The door is not the required exit door.

- The stairway on the exterior side has two or fewer risers.
- The door, other than an exterior storm or screen door, does not swing over the stairway.

Note: The maximum slope for exterior landings is ¼:12 (2%).

Note: The code does not require a 36 in. landing for exterior balconies that are smaller than 60 sq. ft. that are only accessible from the inside.

Stairways

The code addresses stair safety through provisions for proper pitch, walking surface, clearances, uniformity, and graspable handrails. The provisions only apply to stairways within or serving a building, porch or deck. Stairways leading to crawl spaces and uninhabitable attics are exempt.

Stairway Width and Headroom

As part of the egress path, the IRC establishes minimum dimensions for width and headroom height for a safe stairway. The minimum clear width is greater above the handrails to accommodate a person's shoulder width. Headroom is measured vertically above the nose of the tread. The dimension requirements are as follows:

- Clear width above the handrail is at least 36 in.
- Handrail projection is not more than 4½ in. on each side.
- The minimum clear width at and below the handrail is
  - 31½ in. if there is handrail on one side
  - 27 in. if there is handrail on both sides
- Headroom must be at least 6 ft. 8 in.

Stair Treads and Risers

The minimum tread depth and maximum riser height determine the maximum stair steepness but just as important for stair safety is the uniformity of treads and risers for the full *flight* of the stairs (fig. 3.2). The requirements are

- A maximum riser height of no more than 7¾ in.
- No more than ⅜ in. tolerance between the largest and smallest riser.
- A minimum tread depth of 10 in.
- No more than ⅜ in. tolerance between the largest and the smallest tread.
- Winder treads must be at least 10 in. deep at 1 ft. in from the narrow side and not less than 6 in. at any point.

Figure 3.2 Stair tread and riser detail

Stair Profile

In most cases, the IRC requires solid risers and tread nosings that project in front of the solid riser. The nosing dimensions are:

- Projection of ¾ to 1¼ in. beyond riser
- Radius not greater than 9/16 in.

Nosings are not required when the tread depth is 11 in. or greater.

Solid risers are not required if one of the following criteria is met:

- The opening between treads does not allow the passage of a 4 in. sphere.
- The opening is not more than 30 in. above the floor or grade.

Landings at Stairways

A floor or landing typically is required at the top and bottom of stairs.

- A landing is not required at the top of interior stairs if a door does not swing over stairs. (This requirement applies to attached garages and other interior stairs.)
- Landings must be at least the width of the stair and 36 in. in the direction of travel.
- No more than a 12 ft. 7 in. rise is permitted between landings.

Handrails

A handrail is required on at least one side of each stair flight with four or more risers. The handrail must comply with these requirements (fig. 3.3):

- Height 34–38 in. above the nose of the tread
- Ends returned to a wall or posts

Figure 3.3 Stair and handrail

- Space of at least 1½ in. between the wall and the handrail
- Continuous for the full flight, from a point above the bottom riser to the top riser
  - Handrails may be interrupted by a newel post at a turn.
  - Volute, turnout, starting easing, or starting newel may be used over the lowest tread or the top landing.

Approved Handrail Grip Sizes

The size and shape of handrails must be suitable for grasping to prevent falls on stairs. The code offers three options for satisfying this requirement as follows (fig. 3.4):

- Circular with a 1¼–2 in. diameter
- Noncircular, perimeter of 4–6¼ in. with a cross section of no more than 2¼ in.
- Noncircular, perimeter more than 6¼ in. with a graspable finger recess area on both sides of the profile
  - Finger-recess depth of at least ⁵⁄₁₆ in.
  - Width of the handrail above the recess, 1¼–2¾ in.

Note: Other shapes that provide equivalent graspability are also acceptable.

Spiral Stairs

Spiral stairways are an exception to the general stair requirements and are permitted, as follows, with no limitation on the area or *habitable space* they serve (fig. 3.5).

- Width at least 26 in.
- At least 6¾ in. tread depth at 12 in. from the narrower edge
- All treads identical
- Risers no more than 9½ in.
- Headroom at least 6 ft. 6 in.

46 2021 HOME BUILDERS' JOBSITE CODES

Figure 3.4 Handrail shapes

continuous handrail with
ends returned to wall

down

min. 36"

Newel post may interrupt
handrails at turns.

up

31 1/2"
min.

36"

Winder detail

min. 10"

12"

min. 6"

Figure 3.5 Winder treads

Ramps

As is the case for stairs, handrails, guards, and other
elements, the IRC governs only ramps that are
within or serving a building, porch or deck. Separate
elements such as landscaping features, including
stairs, ramps, sidewalks, and driveways, are not
regulated by the code. The code limits the slope of
ramps as follows:

- Maximum 1:8 (12.5%) slope for ramps that do
  not serve the required egress door
- Maximum 1:12 (8.3%) slope for ramps serving the
  required egress door

*Note: Ramps serving the required egress door may have
a slope of up to 1:8 (12.5%) if site constraints prohibit a
1:12 slope.*

- 3 × 3 ft. landings at the following locations:
  - Top and bottom of ramps
  - Where doors open onto ramps
  - Where ramps change direction
- Handrails on at least one side of all ramps exceed-
  ing a slope of 1:12 (8.3% slope).

Guards

To protect against falls and injury, the code requires
guards at the edges of elevated walking surfaces that

are more than 30 in. above the floor or ground at any point within 36 in. of the edge of the walking surface (figs. 3.6 and 3.7).

Guard Height
When the code requires a guard, the minimum guard height is

- 36 in. above the walking surface of decks, balconies, porches, landings, floors, and ramps
- 34 in. above the tread nosing on the open sides of stairs

Figure 3.6 Determining required guard locations

Figure 3.7 Guard dimensions

Guard Openings

The code limits the size of any openings in balusters or other infill components of required guards to prevent passage of the following:

■ 4 in. diameter sphere at most locations
■ 4⅜ in. diameter sphere at the sides of stairs
■ 6 in. diameter sphere at the triangle formed by the riser, tread, and bottom rail of a guard at the open side of a stairway

Window Sill Height

To reduce injuries to children from falls through windows, the code requires the lowest part of the clear opening of the window to be at least 24 in. above the finished floor if the window opening is more than 72 in. above the grade or surface below (fig. 3.8). If the opening is less than 24 in. in these locations, installation can include a barrier or limits on the window dimensions as follows:

■ Openings in operable portions of windows that do not allow passage of a 4-in.-diameter sphere
■ Approved window opening control device
■ Approved window fall-prevention device

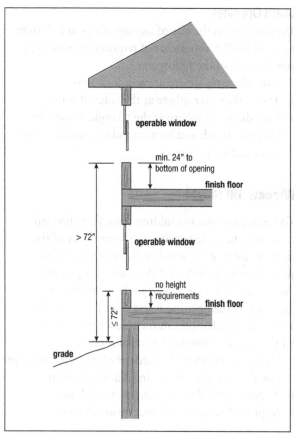

Figure 3.8 Window sill height

Carbon Monoxide Alarms

The code requires carbon monoxide alarms as follows:

Required Locations

In new homes and dwelling units undergoing remodeling, the code requires a carbon monoxide alarm outside each separate sleeping area.

Note: An alarm is also required in a bedroom if the bedroom or attached bathroom contains a fuel-burning appliance.

Note: Dwelling units without an attached garage and with no fuel-fired appliances do not require carbon monoxide alarms.

Installation Requirements

The carbon monoxide alarms must meet the following installation requirements:

- Connected to the building power with no disconnection switch
- Battery backup
- Intetconnection if the dwelling requires more than one alarm

Additions, Alterations, and Repairs

For construction that requires a permit, other than deck and porch additions and exterior work, such as siding, windows, doors, and roofing, dwelling units must have carbon monoxide alarms located as required for new construction. However, the carbon monoxide alarms may be battery operated without connection to the building wiring.

Note: The code requires interconnection of multiple alarms if the remodeling work provides access for the interconnection wiring.

Light, Ventilation, Heating

The code sets minimum requirements for natural or artificial light, fresh air ventilation, and heating in cold climates, to create a healthy and livable environment.

Light

In almost all cases, electric lighting satisfies the minimum illumination requirement of 6 *footcandles* for habitable rooms and bathrooms. However, windows may still be required for ventilation and emergency escape and rescue. Interior and exterior stairs require artificial lighting to illuminate the landings and treads. The light source must be located

- To illuminate interior landings and treads to a minimum level of 1 footcandle
- In the immediate vicinity of the top landing at exterior locations

■ At the bottom landing of exterior stairs leading to a basement

For lighting that is not continuous or automatic, the code requires control by a switch located at each floor level for interior stairs with six or more risers

Ventilation

Homes that comply with the energy efficiency provisions of the code are of sufficiently tight construction to require mechanical ventilation to bring in fresh air. Although openable windows are still desirable for a healthy living environment, the IRC requires a *whole-house mechanical ventilation system* (or other approved means of mechanical ventilation) when the air infiltration rate is within the limits set by the energy requirements in the dwelling unit as determined by a blower door test. As part of this system, bathrooms typically have local exhaust (an exhaust fan) and openable windows are optional. Outside air intake openings must be

■ At least 10 ft. from any noxious source, such as plumbing vents or chimneys

■ Protected on the outside with corrosion-resistant screens with an opening of ¼ in. to ½ in.

Heating

Dwellings must incorporate heating where the winter design temperature, as determined by the local jurisdiction, is less than 60ºF. All habitable rooms must be capable of maintaining a minimum temperature of 68ºF at 3 ft. above the floor and 2 ft. from exterior walls.

Minimum Room Dimensions

Minimum dimensions and areas for rooms and hallways are as follows:

- Habitable rooms except kitchens, at least 70 sq. ft., with a minimum dimension of 7 ft.
- Hallway width, at least 3 ft.

Minimum ceiling height measured from the finished floor is 7 ft. except as follows:

- Sloped ceiling, 7 ft. for 50% of required area
- Bathrooms and laundry rooms, 6 ft. 8 in.
- In showers, 6 ft. 8 in.
- Basements with no habitable space, 6 ft. 8 in.
  Note: *Beams and ducts may be 6 ft. 4 in. from the floor in basements. For areas other than basements, beams may be 6 ft. 6 in. above the floor when spaced apart at least 36 inches.*

Sanitation

Minimum sanitary requirements for each dwelling unit are as follows:

- Connection to approved water supply and approved sewer or private septic system
- One water closet, lavatory, and bathtub or shower
- Kitchen with sink
- Hot and cold water to sinks, lavatories, laundry, bathtubs, and showers

Toilet, Bath, and Shower Spaces

Showers must have nonabsorbent wall surfaces to 6 ft. above the floor. They must be at least 30 × 30 in. with 24 in. in front of opening. Other minimum clearances for bathroom fixtures are as follows (fig. 3.9):

- 21 in. in front of water closet and lavatory
- 15 in. from centerline of water closet or lavatory to wall, vanity cabinet, or tub
- 30 in. from centerline of lavatory to centerline of water closet
  Note: The code permits a narrow shower space of 25 in. or more when the area of the shower is not less than 1,300 sq. in. (for example, 25 in. × 52 in.)

Figure 3.9 Minimum bathroom fixture clearances

Safety Glazing

When glazing is installed in hazardous locations where human impact could occur, the code requires safety glazing, such as tempered or laminated glass. In most cases, the glazing must be etched or permanently *labeled* to identify the type of glazing and the safety glazing standard with which it complies. The code defines the following locations with glazing as hazardous and, therefore, requires safety glazing (fig. 3.10):

- Fixed and operable panels of all swinging, sliding, and bifold doors
- Within 24 in. of the operable panel of a door in a closed position and where the glazing's bottom edge is less than 60 in. above the floor, unless
  - There is an intervening wall.
  - The door is to a closet no more than 3 ft. deep.
  - The wall with glazing is perpendicular to the closed door and the door does not swing toward the glazing.
- Guards and railings.

Figure 3.10 Safety glazing

- In enclosures of or adjacent to hot tubs, spas, whirlpools, bathtubs, showers, and swimming pools where the bottom exposed edge of the glazing is less than 60 in. above any standing or walking surface. (fig. 3.11)
- Wherever there is an individual pane larger than 9 sq. ft. with its bottom edge less than 18 in. above the floor, and its top edge more than 36 in. above the floor
- Less than 36 in. above the walking surface and adjacent to stairways, ramps and intermediate landings between flights

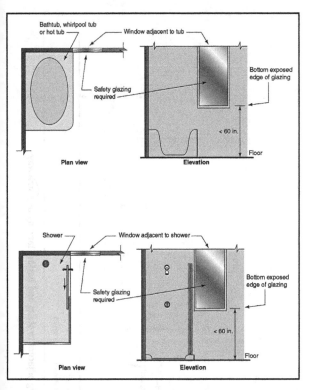

Figure 3.11 Glazing adjacent to tubs and showers

SG = Safety glazing required

NR = Not required to be safety glazing

Figure 3.12 Glazing adjacent to stairs and bottom landing of a stairway

■ Less than 36 in. above the walking surface of the bottom landing and within 60 in. horizontally of the bottom tread of a stairway (fig. 3.12)

Mirrors and other glass panels mounted or hung on a surface that provides a continuous backing support do not require safety glazing. Louvered windows or *jalousies* must meet certain dimension and material requirements but they also do not require safety glazing.

Skylights

A skylight must have approved glazing materials, and in unusual circumstances a special broken glass retention screen. Laminated glass larger than 16 sq. ft. or more than 12 ft. above the floor requires an interlayer thickness of 0.030 in. but does not require a broken glass retention screen. Fully tempered glass without a broken glass retention screen is limited to either of the following conditions:

■ Glass area no more than 16 sq. ft., with the highest point of the glass no more than 12 ft. above a walking surface, nominal glass thickness less than or equal to ³⁄₁₆ in., and any outboard panes fully tempered, laminated, or wired glass or

■ Glass area greater than 16 sq. ft., sloped no more than 30 degrees from vertical (very steep slope),

with highest point of glass no more than 10 ft. abov
a walking surface

Protecting Wood from Decay

Locations subject to decay require naturally durable
wood or wood treated with preservatives. The heart-
woods of redwood and cedar are considered naturally
durable and decay-resistant. Preservative treatment
must comply with the American Wood Protection
Association (AWPA) standards and be listed for the
use. Lumber and plywood that is preservative treated
must bear an approved quality mark. The following
locations require protection from decay:

- Wood joists less than 18 in. or wood girders less
  than 12 in. above exposed ground in crawl spaces
- Wood sills and framing on concrete or masonry foun
  dation walls less than 8 in. above exposed ground
- Plates on a concrete slab that is in direct contact
  with the ground without a moisture barrier
- Wood girders entering exterior masonry or concrete
  walls with clearances of less than ½ in. between the
  wood and the masonry or concrete on tops, sides,
  and ends of the girder
- Exterior wood siding, sheathing, and wall framing
  with less than 6 in. clearance from the ground or
  less than 2 in. above concrete slabs exposed to the
  weather

- Wood furring strips attached directly to the interior of exterior masonry or concrete walls below grade, except where an approved vapor retarder is applied between the wall and the furring strips
- Wood structural members exposed to the weather and supporting buildings, balconies or porches
  Note: An exception allows typical sawn lumber for geographical regions where decay resistance is not needed because of favorable climatic conditions.
- Wood columns in contact with basement floor slabs unless supported by concrete piers not less than 1 inch above the floor and separated from the concrete pier by a moisture barrier.

Ground Contact
Pressure-preservative-treated wood suitable for ground contact is required for structural supports in the following three locations (naturally durable wood is not permitted):
- In contact with the ground
- Embedded in concrete in contact with the ground
- Embedded in concrete exposed to the weather

Fasteners
Fasteners for pressure-preservative-treated wood shall be of hot-dipped, zinc-coated galvanized steel, stainless steel, silicon bronze, or copper. Such protection

is not required for steel bolts of ½ in. diameter or larger, such as foundation anchor bolts.

Protection Against Termites

In areas subject to termite damage, wood structural elements must be protected by one or more of the following methods:

- Chemical termite treatment
- Termite-baiting system
- Pressure-preservative-treated wood
- Naturally durable termite-resistant wood
- Physical barriers (shields placed on top of exterior foundation walls are permitted only in combination with another method of protection)

Foam Plastic Protection

In likely termite infestation areas, the code prohibits the installation of foam plastics on foundations below grade. At least 6 in. clearance between foam plastics installed above grade and exposed earth is required. An approved method of protecting the foam plastic and structure from subterranean termite damage may be used as an alternative. These protection measures do not apply to the interior side of basement walls.

4

Foundations

The IRC contains prescriptive foundation designs to safely support building loads and transmit those loads to the soil. Builders should pay particular attention to the soil's characteristics and bearing capacity. The code bases footing size on soil-bearing capacity and the average gravity loads (dead, live, and snow) to be supported. As the load-bearing pressure of the soil decreases, footing size increases to distribute the load to a greater area. Fill soils that support footings and foundations must be designed, installed, and tested according to accepted engineering practices.

Soils

When local records indicate that the building site is likely to have expansive, compressible, shifting soil, or other questionable soil characteristics that might damage the structure, the building official may require a test to determine the soil's characteristics.

When a complete geotechnical evaluation is not required and not performed, the code assumes the load-bearing values in table 4.1. Highly organic soils (laden with decayed material from plants), clays, silts, and peat are not included in the table. They require geotechnical analysis and, along with other expansive soils, require an engineered foundation design in accordance with the IBC.

Concrete

The compressive strength of concrete is expressed in pounds per square inch (psi) after 28 days curing time. The code requires concrete to have a minimum compressive strength of 2,500 psi for most applications (table 4.2). Stronger concrete, often including entrained air, is specified in geographic areas subject to moderate or severe weathering potential when the concrete is exposed to the weather or is for a garage floor slab.

Footings

Unless an approved alternative method is used, the code typically requires continuous concrete footings to support exterior walls. The number of stories supported, the load-bearing value of the soil, the snow

Table 4.1 Presumptive load-bearing values and properties of soils

Unified soil classification system symbol	Soil description	Load bearing pressure (psf)	Drainage	Frost heave potential	Volume change potential expansion
GW	Well-graded gravels, gravel-sand mixtures, little or no fines	3,000	Good	Low	Low
GP	Poorly graded gravels or gravel-sand mixtures, little or no fines	3,000	Good	Low	Low
SW	Well-graded sands, gravelly sands, little or no fines	2,000	Good	Low	Low
SP	Poorly graded sands or gravelly sands, little or no fines	2,000	Good	Low	Low
GM	Silty gravels, gravel-sand-silt mixtures	2,000	Good	Medium	Low
SM	Silty sand, sand-silt mixtures	2,000	Good	Medium	Low
GC	Clayey gravels, gravel-sand-clay mixtures	2,000	Medium	Medium	Low

(continued)

Table 4.1 Presumptive load-bearing values and properties of soils (*continued*)

Unified soil classification system symbol	Soil description	Load bearing pressure (psf)	Drainage	Frost heave potential	Volume change potential expansion
SC	Clayey sands, sand-clay mixture	2,000	Medium	Medium	Low
ML	Inorganic silts and very fine sands, rock flour, silty or clayey fine sands or clayey silts with slight plasticity	1,500	Medium	High	Low
CL	Inorganic clays of low to medium plasticity, gravelly clays, sandy clays, silty clays, lean clays	1,500	Medium	Medium	Medium to Low
CH	Inorganic clays of high plasticity, fat clays	1,500	Poor	Medium	High
MH	Inorganic silts, micaceous or diatomaceous fine sandy or silty soils, elastic silts	1,500	Poor	High	High

Table 4.2 Minimum specified compressive strength of concrete

Type or location of concrete construction	Minimum specified compressive strength at 28 days in psi		
	Weathering potential		
	Negligible	Moderate	Severe
Basement walls, foundations, and other concrete not exposed to the weather	2,500	2,500	2,500*
Basement slabs and interior slabs on grade, except garage floor slabs	2,500	2,500	2,500*
Basement walls, foundation walls, exterior walls, and other vertical concrete work exposed to the weather	2,500	3,000†	3,000†
Porches, carport slabs, and steps exposed to the weather, and garage floor slabs	2,500	3,000†	3,500†

*Concrete subject to freezing and thawing during construction shall be air-entrained.
†Concrete shall be air-entrained.

load, the type of construction and the type of foundation determine the minimum width and thickness of spread footings (table 4.3). The minimum footing thickness (T) is 6 in. but this thickness increases when the footing projection (P)—the distance from the edge of the footing to the edge of the foundation wall it is supporting—exceeds 6 in. (P cannot exceed T). The soil type and total tributary load determine pier and column footing sizes (total load/psf soil bearing pressure = minimum sq. ft. of footing).

Table 4.3 Minimum width and thickness for concrete footings (in.)

Light-frame construction

Story and type of structure	Load-bearing value of soil (psf)					
	1500	2000	2500	3000	3500	4000
1 story–slab-on-grade	12 × 6	12 × 6	12 × 6	12 × 6	12 × 6	12 × 6
1 story–with crawl space	13 × 6	12 × 6	12 × 6	12 × 6	12 × 6	12 × 6
1 story–plus basement	16 × 6	12 × 6	12 × 6	12 × 6	12 × 6	12 × 6
2 story–slab-on-grade	13 × 6	12 × 6	12 × 6	12 × 6	12 × 6	12 × 6
2 story–with crawl space	16 × 6	12 × 6	12 × 6	12 × 6	12 × 6	12 × 6
2 story–plus basement	19 × 6	14 × 6	12 × 6	12 × 6	12 × 6	12 × 6
3 story–slab-on-grade	16 × 6	14 × 6	12 × 6	12 × 6	12 × 6	12 × 6
3 story–with crawl space	19 × 6	14 × 6	12 × 6	12 × 6	12 × 6	12 × 6
3 story–plus basement	22 × 7	16 × 6	13 × 6	12 × 6	12 × 6	12 × 6

Light-frame construction with brick veneer

Story and type of structure	Load-bearing value of soil (psf)					
	1500	2000	2500	3000	3500	4000
1 story–slab-on-grade	13 × 6	12 × 6	12 × 6	12 × 6	12 × 6	12 × 6
1 story–with crawl space	15 × 6	12 × 6	12 × 6	12 × 6	12 × 6	12 × 6
1 story–plus basement	18 × 6	14 × 6	12 × 6	12 × 6	12 × 6	12 × 6
2 story–slab-on-grade	18 × 6	14 × 6	12 × 6	12 × 6	12 × 6	12 × 6
2 story–with crawl space	20 × 6	15 × 6	12 × 6	12 × 6	12 × 6	12 × 6
2 story–plus basement	24 × 9	15 × 6	14 × 6	12 × 6	12 × 6	12 × 6
3 story–slab-on-grade	23 × 6	18 × 6	14 × 6	12 × 6	12 × 6	12 × 6
3 story–with crawl space	26 × 9	19 × 6	15 × 6	13 × 6	12 × 6	12 × 6
3 story–plus basement	29 × 11	22 × 7	17 × 6	14 × 6	12 × 6	12 × 6

Note: *Values are based on a snow load of 30 psf*

Footing Placement

To protect a building's structural integrity, footings must meet the following conditions (fig. 4.1):

- Bear on undisturbed natural soils or engineered fill
- Be located at least 12 in. below undisturbed ground for exterior footings
- Not bear on frozen soil (unless frozen condition is permanent)
- Be below frost depth (unless there is a frost-protected shallow foundation system)
- Have a slope of 10% or less on the bottom of the footing

Note: The minimum width W is based on the soil bearing values in table 4.1 and the conditions in table 4.3. The footing projection P must be at least 2 in. and shall not exceed the footing thickness.

Frost protection is not required for the following structures:

- Light-framed accessory buildings of 600 sq. ft. or less, with an eave height of not more than 10 ft.
- Other accessory buildings of 400 sq. ft. or less with an eave height of not more than 10 ft.
- Decks not supported by a dwelling

Figure 4.1 Concrete foundation detail

Source: 2006 International Residential Code Study Companion. Washington, DC: International Code Council, 2006. p.113.

Note: The minimum width W is based on the soil bearing values in table 4.1 and the conditions in table 4.3. The footing projection P must be at least 2 in. and shall not exceed the footing thickness.

Concrete and Masonry Foundation Walls

The IRC provides prescriptive designs for cast-in-place concrete, precast concrete, and concrete masonry unit foundations supporting light-frame construction.

Cast-in-place Concrete Foundations

In general, the provisions for wall thickness, height, and reinforcement are the same for removable form and stay-in-place form concrete walls. Concrete basement walls must be supported laterally at the top and bottom before backfilling. The amount of vertical reinforcement is based on the following:

- Wall thickness
- Wall height
- Unbalanced backfill height
- Soil type

The minimum amount of horizontal reinforcing steel for cast-in-place concrete basement walls is one No. 4 bar at the top of the wall and the following:

- One No. 4 bar near mid-height of basement walls not more than 8 ft. high
  or
- One No. 4 bar near the ⅓ points of basement walls more than 8 ft. high

The code places additional limits on concrete walls located in Seismic Design Categories D_0, D_1, and D_2.

Precast Concrete Foundation Walls

Precast foundations are engineered systems that are manufactured in a controlled environment in various profiles including stud-and-cavity, and solid, composite, and hollow-core panels. They require concrete with a higher compressive strength. Precast foundations must be installed according to the manufacturer's instructions. The code prescribes the following footings:

- Concrete or solid masonry with continuous non-shrink grout
  or
- Compacted crushed stone (permitted in Seismic Design Categories A, B, and C)

The code provides tables for sizing crushed stone footings.

Masonry Foundation Walls

The code limits masonry foundation walls without reinforcing to 9 ft. or less, depending on the soil type, masonry thickness, and grouting of hollow units. The code generally does not permit masonry without reinforcing in Seismic Design Categories D_0, D_1, and D_2. Masonry basement walls must be laterally supported at the top and bottom before backfilling. The minimum amount of vertical reinforcement for masonry basement walls is based on

- Nominal masonry thickness of 8, 10, or 12 in.
- Wall height
- Unbalanced backfill height
- Soil type

The code places additional requirements on masonry walls located in Seismic Design Categories D_0, D_1, and D_2.

Surface and Foundation Drainage

Moving water away from the foundation is important to prevent moisture damage to a structure.

Grading for Surface Drainage

The IRC sets minimum grade requirements to adequately drain surface water. Concrete and masonry foundation walls must extend above the finished grade at least as high as follows:

- 6 in. when supporting wood frame walls
- 4 in. where the construction is masonry veneer over wood frame walls

Lots must be graded to drain surface water away from foundation walls to a storm sewer or other approved point of collection. Generally, grade must fall a minimum of 6 in. within the first 10 ft. from the building. When distances to property lines or other lot characteristics prohibit the prescribed slope, the code permits construction of swales or drains and does not specify a minimum slope.

Foundation Drainage

Drains are required around foundations that enclose habitable or usable spaces located below grade (fig. 4.2). Approved drainage systems must
- Be installed at or below the area to be protected
- Discharge by gravity or mechanical means to an approved location

Drainage tiles or perforated pipe must be
- Placed on at least 2 in. of washed gravel
- Covered with at least 6 in. of washed gravel

Note: Perforated pipe requires a filter membrane around the pipe or over the gravel cover.

Gravel or crushed stone drains must
- Extend 12 in. beyond the edge of the footing
- Extend 6 in. above the footing
- Be covered with an approved filter membrane

Note: No drainage system is required when the foundation is installed on well-drained ground or sand-gravel mixture soils.

Figure 4.2 Foundation drain

Dampproofing and Waterproofing

Approved coatings or membranes must be applied
to the exterior of basement walls to prevent moisture
penetration.

■ Concrete and masonry foundations that enclose
   interior spaces and floors below grade must be
   dampproofed with approved materials from the
   top of the footing to the finished grade.
■ Areas with a high water table or other known
   severe soil-water conditions require waterproofing.

Under-Floor Space

The code stipulates certain moisture control and
access requirements for enclosed under-floor spaces,
commonly referred to as crawl spaces.

Crawl Space Ventilation

The IRC prescribes the location and screening
requirements for ventilation openings through
foundation walls or exterior walls as follows:

■ Install one ventilation opening within 3 ft. of
   each corner.
■ Cover openings with approved vent, mesh, or
   screen materials.

The total net area of ventilation openings is as follows:

- With vapor retarder on ground surface, at least 1 sq. ft. for each 1,500 sq. ft. of area
- Without vapor retarder, at least 1 sq. ft. for each 150 sq. ft. of area

Unvented Crawl Space

For an unvented crawl space, the code requires the following:

- A vapor retarder cover on top of exposed earth
- Vapor retarder sealed to the stem wall
- Continuous mechanical exhaust ventilation or conditioned air supply provided
- Insulation installed on exterior walls

Note: The code also permits dehumidification of the crawl space in lieu of mechanical ventilation or conditioned air supply.

Access to Crawl Space

- Access openings through the floor must be at least 18 × 24 in.
- Openings through a perimeter wall must be at least 16 × 24 in.

5

Floors

This chapter addresses load-bearing requirements and floor framing details for wood floor framing, cantilevers, the use of wood structural panel floor sheathing, details for ground-level concrete floors, fire protection of light-frame construction, draft stopping and deck construction.

Wood Floor Framing

Load-bearing dimension lumber for joists, beams, and girders must be identified by a grade mark. The intended use of the floor space, grade and species of lumber, and dead load in accordance with the appropriate span table determine allowable joist spans. For sleeping areas, habitable attics, and attics accessed by fixed stairs, the minimum live load is 30 psf. Other floor joists must be sized to carry a live load of not less than 40 psf. Floors of conventional wood frame construction typically assume a dead load of 10 psf. For heavier flooring materials, joists may need to support a dead load of 20 psf. Allowable deflection for floor joists is limited to the length divided by 360 (L/360), as discussed in chapter 1. The joist spacing and spans (tables 5.1 and 5.2) account for this deflection.

Cantilever Joists for Wood Floor Framing

The code permits using prescriptive tables to determine the maximum span for floor cantilever joists when the joists support

- A light-frame bearing wall and roof only
- An exterior balcony

Table 5.3 assumes No. 2 grade of Douglas fir-larch, hem-fir, spruce-pine-fir, or southern pine for repetitive (3 or more) members. Uplift at the back span and connections capable of resisting the uplift forces also must be considered. The code requires a full-depth rim joist at the cantilevered end of the joists and solid blocking at the cantilever support.

Table 5.4 assumes No. 2 grade of Douglas fir-larch, hem-fir, spruce-pine-fir, or southern pine for repetitive (3 or more) members. The ratio of back span to cantilever must be at least 2:1. Uplift at the back span and connections capable of resisting the uplift forces also must be considered. The code requires a full-depth rim joist at the cantilevered end of the joists and solid blocking at the cantilever support.

Girders

Tables 6.4 and 6.5 in chapter 6 provide allowable spans for girders and headers fabricated of dimension lumber and located in an exterior or interior bearing wall. These tables

- Provide the required number of jack studs to support each end
- Consider the overall width of the building and the elements being supported in determining spans.
- Include values for ground snow loads of 30, 50, and 70 psf

Wood Floor Framing Details

Floor framing, including joists, headers, beams, and girders, shall be positively fastened to transfer all loads to the foundation and ensure against uplift and lateral displacement.

Joists Under Bearing Partitions

The IRC provides specific details for joists supporting bearing partitions as follows:

- Joists under parallel bearing partitions must be adequate to support the load.

Table 5.1 Floor joist spans for common lumber species, #2 grade

(residential sleeping areas, live load = 30 psf, L/360)

Joist spacing (in.)	Species	Dead load = 10 psf			
		2 × 6	2 × 8	2 × 10	2 × 12
		Maximum floor joist spans			
		(ft.-in.)	(ft.-in.)	(ft.-in.)	(ft.-in.)
12	Douglas fir-larch	11-10	15-7	19-10	23-4
	Hem-fir	11-0	14-6	18-6	22-6
	Southern pine	11-3	14-11	18-1	21-4
	Spruce-pine-fir	11-3	14-11	19-0	23-0
16	Douglas fir-larch	10-9	14-2	17-5	20-3
	Hem-fir	10-0	13-2	16-10	19-8
	Southern pine	10-3	13-3	15-8	18-6
	Spruce-pine-fir	10-3	13-6	17-2	19-11
19.2	Douglas fir-larch	10-1	13-0	15-11	18-6
	Hem-fir	9-5	12-5	15-6	17-1
	Southern pine	9-6	12-1	14-4	16-10
	Spruce-pine-fir	9-8	12-9	15-8	18-3
24	Douglas fir-larch	9-3	11-8	14-3	16-6
	Hem-fir	8-9	11-4	13-10	16-1
	Southern pine	8-6	10-10	12-10	15-1
	Spruce-pine-fir	8-11	11-6	14-1	16-3

Table 5.1 Floor joist spans for common lumber species, #2 grade (*continued*)

(residential sleeping areas, live load = 30 psf, L/360)

Joist spacing (in.)	Species	Dead load = 20 psf			
		2 × 6	2 × 8	2 × 10	2 × 12
		Maximum floor joist spans			
		(ft.-in.)	(ft.-in.)	(ft.-in.)	(ft.-in.)
12	Douglas fir-larch	11-8	14-9	18-0	20-11
	Hem-fir	11-0	14-4	17-6	20-4
	Southern pine	10-9	13-8	16-2	19-1
	Spruce-pine-fir	11-3	14-7	17-9	20-7
16	Douglas fir-larch	10-1	12-9	15-7	18-1
	Hem-fir	9-10	12-5	15-2	17-7
	Southern pine	9-4	11-10	14-0	16-6
	Spruce-pine-fir	9-11	12-7	15-5	17-10
19.2	Douglas fir-larch	9-3	11-8	14-3	16-6
	Hem-fir	8-11	11-4	13-10	16-1
	Southern pine	8-6	10-10	12-10	15-1
	Spruce-pine-fir	9-1	11-6	14-1	16-3
24	Douglas fir-larch	8-3	10-5	12-9	14-9
	Hem-fir	8-0	10-2	12-5	14-4
	Southern pine	7-7	9-8	11-5	13-6
	Spruce-pine-fir	8-1	10-3	12-7	14-7

Table 5.2 Floor joist spans for common lumber species, #2 grade

(residential living areas, live load = 40 psf, L/360)

Joist spacing (in.)	Species and grade	Dead load = 10 psf			
		2 × 6	2 × 8	2 × 10	2 × 12
		Maximum floor joist spans			
		(ft.-in.)	(ft.-in.)	(ft.-in.)	(ft.-in.)
12	Douglas fir-larch	10-9	14-2	18-0	20-11
	Hem-fir	10-0	13-2	16-10	20-4
	Southern pine	10-3	13-6	16-2	19-1
	Spruce-pine-fir	10-3	13-6	17-3	20-7
16	Douglas fir-larch	9-9	12-9	15-7	18-1
	Hem-fir	9-1	12-0	15-2	17-7
	Southern pine	9-4	11-10	14-0	16-6
	Spruce-pine-fir	9-4	12-3	15-5	17-10
19.2	Douglas fir-larch	9-2	11-8	14-3	16-6
	Hem-fir	8-7	11-3	13-10	16-1
	Southern pine	8-6	10-10	12-10	15-1
	Spruce-pine-fir	8-9	11-6	14-1	16-3
24	Douglas fir-larch	8-3	10-5	12-9	14-9
	Hem-fir	7-11	10-2	12-5	14-4
	Southern pine	7-7	9-8	11-5	13-6
	Spruce-pine-fir	8-1	10-3	12-7	14-7

Table 5.2 Floor joist spans for common lumber species, #2 grade (*continued*)

(residential living areas, live load = 40 psf, L/360)

Joist spacing (in.)	Species and grade	Dead load = 20 psf			
		2 × 6	2 × 8	2 × 10	2 × 12
		Maximum floor joist spans			
		(ft.-in.)	(ft.-in.)	(ft.-in.)	(ft.-in.)
12	Douglas fir-larch	10-8	13-6	16-5	19-1
	Hem-fir	10-0	13-1	16-0	18-6
	Southern pine	9-10	12-6	14-9	17-5
	Spruce-pine-fir	10-3	13-3	16-3	18-10
16	Douglas fir-larch	9-3	11-8	14-3	16-6
	Hem-fir	8-11	11-4	13-10	16-1
	Southern pine	8-6	10-10	12-10	15-1
	Spruce-pine-fir	9-1	11-6	14-1	16-3
19.2	Douglas fir-larch	8-5	10-8	13-0	15-1
	Hem-fir	8-2	10-4	12-8	14-8
	Southern pine	7-9	9-10	11-8	13-9
	Spruce-pine-fir	8-3	10-6	12-10	14-10
24	Douglas fir-larch	7-6	9-6	11-8	13-6
	Hem-fir	7-4	9-3	11-4	13-1
	Southern pine	7-0	8-10	10-5	12-4
	Spruce-pine-fir	7-5	9-5	11-6	13-4

Table 5.3 Cantilever spans for floor joists supporting light-frame exterior bearing wall and roof only (floor live load ≤ 40 psf, roof live load ≤ 20 psf)

Member & spacing (in.)	Maximum cantilever span (in.)											
	Ground snow load											
	≤ 20 psf			30 psf			50 psf			70 psf		
	Roof width			Roof width			Roof width			Roof width		
	24 ft	32 ft	40 ft	24 ft	32 ft	40 ft	24 ft	32 ft	40 ft	24 ft	32 ft	40 ft
2 × 8 @ 12	20	15	–	18	–	–	–	–	–	–	–	–
2 × 10 @ 16	29	21	16	26	18	–	20	–	–	–	–	–
2 × 10 @ 12	36	26	20	34	22	16	26	–	–	19	–	–
2 × 12 @ 16	–	32	25	36	29	21	29	20	–	23	19	–
2 × 12 @ 12	–	42	31	–	37	27	36	27	17	31	19	–
2 × 12 @ 8	–	48	45	–	48	38	–	40	26	36	29	18

Note: Spans are based on No. 2 grade lumber of Douglas fir-larch, hem-fir, and spruce-pine-fir for repetitive (three or more) members. No.1 or better shall be used for southern pine.

Table 5.4 Cantilever spans for floor joists supporting exterior balcony

Member size	Spacing (in.)	Maximum cantilever span (in.)		
		Ground snow load		
		≤ 30 psf	50 psf	70 psf
2 × 8	12	42	39	34
2 × 8	16	36	34	29
2 × 10	12	61	57	49
2 × 10	16	53	49	42
2 × 10	24	43	40	34
2 × 12	16	72	67	57
2 × 12	24	58	54	47

Note: Spans are based on No. 2 Grade lumber of Douglas fir-larch, hem-fir, and spruce-pine-fir for repetitive (three or more) members. No.1 or better shall be used for southern pine.

- Double joists that are separated for installation of piping or vents and under parallel bearing partitions require full-depth solid blocking at 4 ft. O.C.
- Bearing partitions perpendicular to joists shall not be offset by more than the joist depth from supporting girders or walls.

Bearing at End of Each Joist, Beam, or Girder

Joists, beams, and girders must be adequately supported at each end as follows:

- At least 1½ in. on wood or metal
- At least 3 in. on masonry or concrete

Alternative End Bearing Supports

Where the ends of joists do not bear on supporting walls or beams, the IRC allows support by one of the following methods:

- Approved joist hangers
- 1 × 4 ribbon strip, joist nailed to the adjacent stud

Joists Framing from Opposite Sides Over a Bearing Support

Where the ends of joists meet at a bearing support such as an interior beam, the joists must be

- Lapped at least 3 in. and nailed together with at least three 10d face nails
  or
- Spliced by wood or metal plate with strength equal to a nailed lap

Supports for Joists Framing into the Side of a Wood Girder

The code includes two methods of joist support at the sides of girders as follows:

- Approved framing anchors
  or
- 2 × 2 ledger strips

Lateral End Support for Joists
Any of the following methods will meet the IRC requirements for lateral support at the ends of floor joists:
- Full-depth solid blocking not less than 2 in. nominal thickness
- End of joist attached to a full-depth header, band, or rim joist
- End of joist attached to an adjoining stud
- Other approved lateral support to prevent rotation

Header and Trimmer Joist Requirements
For framing openings in the floor system, the code prescribes minimum strength and support requirements for headers, trimmers and tail joists based on the length of the wood framing members.
- Headers longer than 4 ft. must not be less than double members.
- Trimmers supporting headers longer than 4 ft. must not be less than double members.
- Headers and tail joists require hangers or other methods of support at bearing ends.

Cutting, Notching, and Drilling

Notches in lumber joists, rafters, and beams are limited as follows (fig. 5.1):

- Depth of no more than ⅙ the depth of the member (no more than ¼ at ends)
- Length of no more than ⅓ the depth of the member

Note: Notches must not be located in the middle ⅓ of the span.

Holes in joists, rafters, and beams are limited as follows:

- The diameter cannot be more than ⅓ the depth of the member.
- Holes must be located at least 2 in. from the top or bottom of the member.

   Note: Holes must be positioned at least 2 in. away from any other hole or notch.

Cuts, notches, and holes in engineered wood products (trusses, *structural composite lumber,* structural glue-laminated members, or I-joists) are prohibited unless they are

- Permitted by the manufacturer's recommendations or
- Part of a specific designed alteration by a registered design professional

Figure 5.1 Cutting, notching, and drilling

Source: International Residential Code for One- and Two-Family Dwellings, 2006. Washington, DC: International Code Council, 2006, p. 105.

Wood Trusses

Trusses must be designed according to accepted engineering practice and referenced standards and braced in accordance with the individual truss design drawings. Truss design drawings must be

- Submitted to the building official and approved prior to installation
- Delivered to the jobsite with the trusses

Note: Alterations to trusses are prohibited unless approved by a registered design professional.

Draft Stopping

Draft stops are required to divide concealed floor spaces into approximately equal areas of no more than 1,000 sq. ft. These concealed spaces typically are created when a ceiling is applied to the bottom of open-web floor trusses or a ceiling is suspended below the floor joists.

Approved draft-stopping materials include the following:

- ½ in. gypsum board
- ⅜ in. wood structural panels
- ⅜ in. particleboard
- Other approved, adequately supported materials

Steel Floor Framing

The code contains prescriptive requirements for cold-formed steel floor framing applicable to buildings not greater than 40 × 60 ft. and not more than 3 stories high. Use of these code provisions is further limited to sites with an ultimate design wind speed of less than 140 mph in Exposure Category B or C and a maximum ground snow load of 70 psf.

Wood Structural Panel Floor Sheathing

Wood structural panels used for subfloor or combined subfloor/underlayment are typically plywood or oriented strand board (OSB). All panels must bear a grade mark issued by an approved agency. Maximum span ratings for application as roof and floor sheathing are part of this grade mark. For example, a grade mark of $24/16$ would indicate a maximum roof rafter spacing of 24 in. and a maximum floor joist spacing of 16 in.

Combination subfloor/underlayment may have a single number indicating the span rating for floors only. The long dimension of the panel is applied perpendicular to the supports and the span rating is based on continuous panels over two or more spans. Requirements for edge blocking for other than tongue-and-groove structural panels depend on the grade and thickness of the panel and spacing of the supports.

Concrete Floors (on Ground)

Reinforcement must be supported to remain in place from the center to the upper ⅓ of the slab. Slabs must be at least 3.5 in. thick.

- Vegetation, top soil, and foreign material must be removed.
- Slabs below grade require 4-in.-thick sand or gravel base course.
  Note: Sand or gravel base course is not required for well-drained, sand-gravel soils.
- A 10 mil polyethylene sheet or approved vapor retarder must be placed under the slab.
  Note: Garages, carports, unheated accessory structures, unheated storage rooms less than 70 sq. ft. and exterior areas do not require the vapor retarder.

Decks

The IRC provides prescriptive methods for deck construction including footings, posts, beams, floor joists, and attachment to the structure as well as other connection and support details. Decks must support a live load of 40 psf or the ground snow load of the geographic location, whichever is greater.

Deck Footings

The code provides minimum footing sizes for deck posts based on the live or snow load, the tributary area being supported and the soil bearing capacity (table 5.5):

- Tributary area, in square feet, is the portion of deck surface supported by the post and footing
- For other than free-standing decks, footings must extend below frost line

   Note: Footing sizes are based on plain concrete (without reinforcing).

Deck Posts

The code sets the maximum post height for supporting beams of single-level wood-framed decks based on the live or snow load, the tributary area of the deck being supported and the size and species of the wood post (table 5.6).

Posts shall bear on footings and be restrained to prevent lateral displacement by one of the following:

- Manufactured connectors,
   or
- Minimum 12 in. embedment in soil or concrete

Table 5.5 Minimum footing size for decks

Live or Ground Snow Load (psf)	Tributary Area (sq. ft.)	Load Bearing Value of Soil (psf)					
		1500			2000		
		Side of a square footing (in.)	Diameter of a round footing (in.)	Thickness (in.)	Side of a square footing (in.)	Diameter of a round footing (in.)	Thickness (in.)
40	20	10	12	6	9	9	6
	40	14	16	6	12	14	6
	60	17	19	6	15	17	6
	80	20	22	7	17	19	6
50	20	11	13	6	10	11	6
	40	15	17	6	13	15	6
	60	19	21	6	16	18	6
	80	21	24	8	19	21	6
60	20	12	14	6	11	12	6
	40	16	19	6	14	16	8
	60	20	23	7	17	20	6
	80	23	26	9	20	23	7

Table 5.6 Deck post height						
Loads (psf)	**Post species**	**Post size**	**Tributary area (sq. ft.)**			
			20	**40**	60	80
			Maximum deck post height (ft.-in.)			
40 live load	Southern pine	4 × 4	14-0	13-8	11-0	9-5
		4 × 6	14-0	14-0	13-11	12-0
		6 × 6	14-0	14-0	14-0	14-0
		8 × 8	14-0	14-0	14-0	14-0
	Redwood Western cedars Ponderosa pine Red pine	4 × 4	14-0	13-2	10-3	8-1
		4 × 6	14-0	14-0	13-6	11-4
		6 × 6	14-0	14-0	14-0	14-0
		8 × 8	14-0	14-0	14-0	14-0
50 ground snow load	Southern pine	4 × 4	14-0	12-2	9-10	8-5
		4 × 6	14-0	14-0	12-6	10-9
		6 × 6	14-0	14-0	14-0	14-0
		8 × 8	14-0	14-0	14-0	14-0
	Redwood Western cedars Ponderosa pine Red pine	4 × 4	14-0	11-8	9-0	6-10
		4 × 6	14-0	14-0	12-0	10-0
		6 × 6	14-0	14-0	14-0	14-0
		8 × 8	14-0	14-0	14-0	14-0
60 ground snow load	Southern pine	4 × 4	14-0	11-1	8-11	7-7
		4 × 6	14-0	14-0	11-4	9-9
		6 × 6	14-0	14-0	14-0	14-0
		8 × 8	14-0	14-0	14-0	14-0
	Redwood Western cedars Ponderosa pine Red pine	4 × 4	14-0	10-6	7-9	4-7
		4 × 6	14-0	13-7	10-9	8-9
		6 × 6	14-0	14-0	14-0	14-0
		8 × 8	14-0	14-0	14-0	14-0

Deck Beams

The IRC provides the maximum allowable spans for wood deck beams using No. 2 grade of typical lumber species. Spans are based on a live load of 40 psf or the ground snow load for the geographic area, whichever is greater (table 5.7).

The following information applies to wood deck beams:

- Cantilevers limited to one-fourth of the beam span
- Beam plies fastened with two rows of 10d nails at 16 in. O.C along each edge
- Minimum 1½ in. bearing on wood or metal
- Minimum 3 in. bearing on concrete or masonry

Figures 5.2 and 5.3 show two acceptable methods for attaching deck beams to deck posts. The code permits other equivalent means.

Loads (psf)	Beam species	Beam size	Deck joist span length				
			8	10	12	14	16
			Maximum deck beam span length				
40 live load	Southern pine	2 – 2 × 8	7-7	6-9	6-2	5-9	5-4
		2 – 2 × 10	9-0	8-0	7-4	6-9	6-4
		2 – 2 × 12	10-7	9-5	8-7	8-0	7-5
	Redwood Western cedars Ponderosa pine Red pine	2 – 2 × 8	6-10	6-1	5-7	5-2	4-10
		2 – 2 × 10	8-4	7-5	6-9	6-3	5-10
		2 – 2 × 12	9-8	8-7	7-10	7-3	6-10
50 ground snow load	Southern pine	2 – 2 × 8	7-4	6-7	6-0	5-7	5-2
		2 – 2 × 10	8-9	7-10	7-1	6-7	6-2
		2 – 2 × 12	10-3	9-2	8-5	7-9	7-3
	Redwood Western cedars Ponderosa pine Red pine	2 – 2 × 8	6-8	5-11	5-5	5-0	4-8
		2 – 2 × 10	8-2	7-3	6-8	6-2	5-9
		2 – 2 × 12	9-5	8-5	7-8	7-2	6-8
60 ground snow load	Southern pine	2 – 2 × 8	6-10	6-1	5-7	5-2	4-10
		2 – 2 × 10	8-1	7-3	6-7	6-1	5-8
		2 – 2 × 12	9-6	8-6	7-9	7-2	6-9
	Redwood Western cedars Ponderosa pine Red pine	2 – 2 × 8	6-2	5-6	5-0	4-7	4-2
		2 – 2 × 10	7-6	6-9	6-2	5-8	5-4
		2 – 2 × 12	8-9	7-10	7-2	6-7	6-2

Table 5.7 Maximum deck beam span

Figure 5.2 Deck beam to deck post

Figure 5.3 Notched post-to-beam connection

Deck Joists

The IRC provides the maximum allowable spans for wood deck joists using No. 2 grade of typical lumber species. Spans are based on a live load of 40 psf or the ground snow load for the geographic area, whichever is greater (table 5.8).

The following information applies to wood deck joists:

- Cantilevers limited to the value in table 5.8
- Minimum 1½ in. bearing on wood or metal
- Minimum 3 in. bearing on concrete or masonry
- Support by approved joist hangers when framing into the side of a beam

Joists bearing on a beam require connection to resist lateral displacement.

Table 5.8 Maximum deck joist spans

Load (psf)	Joist species	Joist size	Allowable joist span (ft. – in.)			Maximum cantilever (ft. – in.)			
			Joist spacing (in.)			Joist back span (ft.)			
			12	16	24	8	10	12	14
40 live load	Southern pine	2 × 8	13-1	11-10	9-8	2-0	2-6	2-3	NP
		2 × 10	16-2	14-0	11-5	2-0	2-6	3-0	3-4
		2 × 12	18-0	16-6	13-6	2-0	2-6	3-0	3-6
	Redwood Western cedars Ponderosa pine Red pine	2 × 8	11-8	10-7	8-8	2-0	1-11	NP	NP
		2 × 10	14-11	13-0	10-7	2-0	2-6	3-0	2-9
		2 × 12	17-5	15-1	12-4	2-0	2-6	3-0	3-6
50 ground snow load	Southern pine	2 × 8	12-1	11-0	9-5	2-0	2-5	2-3	NP
		2 × 10	15-5	13-9	11-3	2-0	2-6	3-0	3-1
		2 × 12	18-0	16-2	13-2	2-0	2-6	3-0	3-6
	Redwood Western cedars Ponderosa pine Red pine	2 × 8	10-10	9-10	8-6	2-0	1-11	NP	NP
		2 × 10	13-10	12-7	10-5	2-0	2-6	2-9	NP
		2 × 12	16-10	14-9	12-1	2-0	2-6	3-0	3-5
60 ground snow load	Southern pine	2 × 8	11-5	10-4	8-9	2-0	2-4	NP	NP
		2 × 10	14-7	12-9	10-5	2-0	2-6	2-11	2-11
		2 × 12	17-3	15-0	12-3	2-0	2-6	3-0	3-6
	Redwood Western cedars Ponderosa pine Red pine	2 × 8	10-2	9-3	7-11	2-0	1-11	NP	NP
		2 × 10	13-0	11-9	9-7	2-0	2-6	2-7	NP
		2 × 12	15-9	13-8	11-2	2-0	2-6	3-0	3-2

Deck Attachment

The code prescribes one method of attaching a deck ledger to the band or rim joist of the building structure (figs. 5.4 and 5.5). This prescriptive method applies only to the materials specified here:

- 2 × 8 or larger deck ledger of No. 2 preservative-treated lumber or approved decay-resistant lumber
- 2 in. nominal lumber band joist or 1 in. nominal engineered rim board
- Maximum ½ in. wall sheathing
  Note: Maximum 1 in. sheathing is permitted with closer bolt spacing.

For deck attachment using the prescriptive methods, the IRC requires connection to the structure according to table 5.9 and as follows:

- Minimum ½ in. diameter lag screws or bolts with washers
- Hot-dipped galvanized or stainless steel fasteners and washers.
- Lag screws full depth through the joist
- Fasteners staggered along length of ledger
- Fasteners located 2 in. minimum from top of ledger.
- Fasteners located 2 in. minimum from bottom of band joist.
- Fasteners located 2 in. to 5 in. from end of ledger.
- Flashing placed over the ledger.

Other attachment methods must comply with accepted engineering practices.

Figure 5.4 Placement of lag screws and bolts in ledgers

Source: International Residential Code for One-and Two-Family Dwellings, 2012. Washington, DC: International Code Council, 2011, p. 190.

Figure 5.5 Deck ledger connection to structure

Source: International Residential Code for One-and Two-Family Dwellings, 2012. Washington, DC: International Code Council, 2011, p. 190.

Table 5.9 Deck ledger connection to band joist

Load (psf)	Joist span (ft.)	On-center spacing of fasteners		
		1/2-inch diameter lag screw with 1/2-inch maximum sheathing	1/2-inch diameter bolt with 1/2-inch maximum sheathing	1/2-inch diameter bolt with 1-inch maximum sheathing
40 live load	8	23	36	36
	10	18	34	29
	12	15	29	24
	14	13	24	21
50 ground snow load	8	22	36	35
	10	17	33	28
	12	14	27	23
	14	12	23	20
60 ground snow load	8	18	35	30
	10	15	28	24
	12	12	23	20
	14	10	20	17

6

Wall Construction

Conventional light-frame wall construction, with its connections and bracing, must resist the code-prescribed vertical and lateral forces that act on a building, and transfer these loads to the foundation. In addition to setting limits on the size, length, and spacing of studs, the code addresses minimum connection requirements (tables 6.1 and 6.2). It presents a number of methods for wall bracing, which are critical to a building's structural integrity. This chapter also covers the installation of exterior doors and windows.

Wood Wall Framing

The prescriptive provisions of the IRC generally limit stud height in bearing walls to 10 ft. The required size and spacing of studs depend on the number of floors to be supported in addition to the roof (table 6.3).

Table 6.1 Fastening schedule

Item	Description of building elements	Number and type of fastener	Spacing and location
Roof			
1	Blocking between ceiling joists, rafters or trusses to top plate or other framing below	4-8d box (2½" × 0.113"); or 3-8d common (2½" × 0.131"); or 3-10d box (3" × 0.128"); or 3-3" × 0.131" nails	Toe nail
	Blocking between rafters or truss not at the wall top plates, to rafter or truss	2-0d common (2 ½" × 0.131"); or 2-3" × 0.131" nails	Each end toe nail
		2-16d common (3 ½" × 0.162"); or 3-3" × 0.131" nails	End nail
	Flat blocking to truss and web filler	16d common (3½" × 0.162"); or 3" × 0.131" nails	6" o.c. face nail
2	Ceiling joists to top plate	4-8d box (2½" × 0.113"); or 3-8d common (2½" × 0.131"); or 3-10d box (3" × 0.128"); or 3-3" × 0.131" nails	Per joist, toe nail
3	Ceiling joist not attached to parallel rafter, laps over partitions, face nail	4-10d box (3" × 0.128"); or 3-16d common (3½" × 0.162"); or 4-3" × 0.131" nails	Face nail
4	Ceiling joist attached to parallel rafter (heel joint)	Per IRC Table R802.5.1(9)	Face nail
5	Collar tie to rafter, face nail	4-10d box (3" × 0.128"); or 3-10d common (3" × 0.148"); or 4-3" × 0.131" nails	Face nail each rafter

Table 6.1 Fastening schedule *(continued)*

Item	Description of building elements	Number and type of fastener	Spacing and location
Roof *(continued)*			
6	Rafter or roof truss to plate	3-16d box nails (3½" × 0.135"); or 3-10d common nails (3" × 0.148"); or 4-10d box (3" × 0.128"); or 4-3" × 0.131 nails	2 toenails on one side and 1 toenail on opposite side of each rafter or trussi
7	Roof rafters to ridge, valley or hip rafters or roof rafter to minimum 2" ridge beam	4-16d box (3½" × 0.135"); or 3-10d common (3½" × 0.148"); or 4-10d box (3" × 0.128"); or 4-3" × 0.131" nails	Toenail
		3-16d box (3½" × 0.135") 2-16d common (3½" × 0.162"); or 3-10d box (3" × 0.128"); or 3-3" × 0.131" nails	End nail
Wall			
8	Stud to Stud (not at braced wall panels)	16d common (3½" × 0.162")	24" o.c. face nail
		10d box (3" × 0.128"); or 3" × 0.131" nails	16" o.c. face nail
9	Stud to stud and abutting studs at intersecting wall corners (at braced wall panels)	16d box (3½" × 0.135"); or 3" × 0.131" nails	12" o.c. face nail
		16d common (3½" × 0.162")	16" o.c. face nail

(continued)

Table 6.1 Fastening schedule *(continued)*

Item	Description of building elements	Number and type of fastener	Spacing and location
		Wall *(continued)*	
10	Built-up header (2-inch to 2-inch header with ½" spacer)	16d common (3½" × 0.162")	16" o.c. along each edge face nail
		16d box (3½" × 0.135")	12" o.c. along each edge face nail
11	Continuous header to stud	5-8d box (2½" × 0.113"); or 4-8d common (2½" × 0.131"); or 4-10d box (3" × 0.128")	Toe nail
12	Adjacent full-height stud to end of header	4-16d box (3½"× 0.135"); or 3-16d common (3½" × 0.162"); or 4-10d box (3" × 0.128"); or 4-3" × 0.131" nails	End nail
13	Top plate to top plate	16d common (3½" × 0.162")	16" o.c. face nail
		10d common (3" × 0.128"); or 3" × 0.131" nails	12" o.c. face nail
14	Double top plate splice	8-16d common (3½" × 0.162"); or 12-16d box (3½" × 0.135"); or 12-10d box (3" × 0.128"); or 12-3" × 0.131" nails	Face nail on each side of end joint (minimum 24" lap splice length each side of end joint)

Table 6.1 Fastening schedule *(continued)*

Item	Description of building elements	Number and type of fastener	Spacing and location
Wall *(continued)*			
15	Bottom plate to joist, rim joist, band joist or blocking (not at braced wall panels)	16d common (3½" × 0.162")	16" o.c. face nail
		16d box (3½" × 0.135"); or 3" × 0.131" nails	12" o.c. face nail
16	Bottom plate to joist, rim joist, band joist or blocking (at braced wall panel)	3-16d box (3½" × 0.135"); or 2-16d common (3½" × 0.162"); or 4-3" × 0.131" nails	16" o.c. face nail
17	Top or bottom plate to stud	4-8d box (2½" × 0.113");or 3-16d box (3½" × 0.135"); or 4-8d common (2½" × 0.131"); or 4-10d box (3" × 0.128"); or 4-3" × 0.131" nails	Toe nail
		3-16d box (3½" × 0.135"); or 2-16d common (3½" × 0.162"); or 3-10d box (3" × 0.128"); or 3-3" × 0.131" nails	End nail
18	Top plates, laps at corners and intersections	3-10d box (3" × 0.128"); or 2-16d common (3½" × 0.162"); or 3-3" × 0.131" nails	Face nail
19	1" brace to each stud and plate	3-8d box (2½" × 0.113"); or 2-8d common (2½" × 0.131"); or 2-10d box (3" × 0.128") 2 staples 1¾"	Face nail

(continued)

Table 6.1 Fastening schedule *(continued)*

Item	Description of building elements	Number and type of fastener	Spacing and location
Floor			
20	Joist to sill, top plate or girder	4-8d box (2½" × 0.113"); or 3-8d common (2½" × 0.131"); or 3-10d box (3" × 0.128"); or 3-3" × 0.131" nails	Toe nail
21	Rim joist, band joist or blocking to sill or top plate (roof applications also)	8d box (2½" × 0.113")	4" o.c. toe nail
		8d common (2½" × 0.131"); or 10d box (3" × 0.128"); or 3" × 0.131" nails	6" o.c. toe nail
22	Band or Rim Joist to Joist	3-16d common (3½" × 0.162") or 4-10 box (3" × 0.128), or 4-3" × 0.131" nails, or 4-3" × 14 gage staples, ⁷/₁₆" crown	End nail
23	Built-up girders and beams, 2" lumber layers	20d common (4" × 0.192"); or	Nail each layer as follows: 32" o.c. at top and bottom and staggered.
		10d (3" × 0.128"); or 3-3" × 0.131" nails	24" o.c. face nail at top and bottom staggered on opposite sides
		And: 2-20d common (4" × 0.192"); or 3-10d box (3" × 0.128"); or 3-3" × 0.131" nails	Face nail at ends and at each splice

Table 6.1 Fastening schedule *(continued)*

Item	Description of building elements	Number and type of fastener	Edges (in.)	Intermediate Supports (in.)
		Floor *(continued)*		
24	Ledger strip supporting joists or rafters	4-16d box (3½" × 0.135"); or 3-16d common (3½" × 0.162"); or 4-10d box (3" × 0.128"); or 4-3" × 0.131" nails	At each joist or rafter, face nail	
25	Joist to band joist or rim joist	4-10d (3" × 0.128")	End nail	
26	Bridging or blocking to joist	2-10d (3" × 0.128") 2-8d common (2½" × 0.131"); 2-3" × 0.131" nails	Each end, toenail	

Wood structural panels, subfloor, roof and interior wall sheathing to framing, and particleboard wall sheathing to framing

Item		Number and type of fastener	Edges (in.)	Intermediate Supports (in.)
27	³⁄₈"-½"	6d common or deformed (2" × 0.113" × 0.266" head); or 2³⁄₈" × 0.113" × 0.266" head nail (subfloor, wall)	6	6
		8d common (2½" × 0.131") nail (roof) ; or RSRS-01 (2³⁄₈" × 0.113") nail (roof)	6	6

(continued)

Table 6.1 Fastening schedule *(continued)*

Item	Description of building elements	Number and type of fastener	Edges (in.)	Intermediate Supports (in.)
			Spacing of Fasteners	

Wood structural panels, subfloor, roof and interior wall sheathing to framing, and particleboard wall sheathing to framing *(continued)*

Item	Description of building elements	Number and type of fastener	Edges (in.)	Intermediate Supports (in.)
28	19/32"-3/4"	8d common nail (2½" × 0.131" nail (subfloor, wall)	6	12
		8d common (2½" × 0.131") nail (roof); or RSRS-01; (2³/8" × 0.113") nail (roof)	6	6
		Deformed 2³/8" × 0.113" × 0.266" head (wall or subfloor)	6	12
29	7/8"-1¼"	10d common (3" × 0.148") nail or 8d (2½" × 0.131") deformed nail	6	12
	Other wall sheathing			
30	½" structural cellulosic fiberboard sheathing	1½" galvanized roofing nail, 7/16" head diameter; or 1¼" long 16 ga. staple with 7/16" or 1" crown	3	6
31	25/32" structural cellulosic fiberboard sheathing	1¾" galvanized roofing nail; 7/16" head diameter; or 1¼" long 16 ga. staple with 7/16" or 1" crown	3	6

Table 6.1 Fastening schedule *(continued)*

Item	Description of building elements	Number and type of fastener	Spacing of Fasteners Edges (in.)	Inter-mediate Supports (in.)
Other wall sheathing *(continued)*				
32	½" gypsum sheathing	1½" × 0.120" galvanized roofing nail, 7⁄16" head diameter, or 7⁄16" long 16 ga.; staple galvanized, 1½" long; 7⁄16" or 1" crown or 1¼" screws, Type W or S	7	7
33	5⁄8" gypsum sheathing	1¾" × 0.120" galvanized roofing nail, 7⁄16" head diameter, or 1¼" long 16 ga.; staple galvanized, 1½" long; 7⁄16" or 1" crown or 1¼" screws, Type W or S	7	7
Wood structural panels, combination subfloor underlayment to framing				
34	¾" and less	Deformed (2" × 0.113") or Deformed (2" × 0.120") nail; or 8d common (2½" × 0.131") nail	6	12
35	7⁄8"–1"	8d common (2 1/2" × 0.131") nail; or Deformed (2" × 0.113"); or Deformed (2½" × 0.120") nail	6	12
36	1 1⁄8"–1¼"	10d common (3" × 0.148") nail; or Deformed (2" × 0.113"); or Deformed (2½" × 0.120") nail	6	12

Table 6.2 Requirements for wood structural panel wall sheathing used to resist wind pressures

Minimum nail		Minimum wood structural panel span rating	Minimum nominal panel thickness (in.)	Maximum wall stud spacing (in.)	Panel nail spacing		Ultimate design wind speed V$_{ult}$ (mph)		
Size	Penetration (in.)				Edges (in. O.C.)	Field (in. O.C.)	Wind exposure category		
							B	C	D
6d Common (2.0" × 0.113")	1.5	24/0	⅜	16	6	12	140	115	110
8d Common (2.5" × 0.131")	1.75	24/16	7/16	16	6	12	170	140	135
				24	6	12	140	115	110

Table 6.3 Size, height, and spacing of wood studs

Stud size (in.)	Bearing walls					Nonbearing walls	
	Laterally unsupported stud height (ft.)	Maximum spacing when supporting a roof-ceiling assembly or a habitable attic assembly, only (in.)	Maximum spacing when supporting one floor, plus a roof-ceiling assembly or a habitable attic assembly (in.)	Maximum spacing when supporting two floors, plus a roof-ceiling assembly or a habitable attic assembly (in.)	Maximum spacing when supporting one floor only (in.)	Laterally unsupported stud height (ft.)	Maximum spacing (in.)
2 × 3	—	—	—	—	—	10	16
2 × 4	10	24	16	—	24	14	24
3 × 4	10	24	24	16	24	14	24
2 × 5	10	24	24	—	24	16	24
2 × 6	10	24	24	16	24	20	24

Note: A habitable attic assembly supported by 2" × 4" studs is limited to a roof span of 32 ft. Where the roof span exceeds 32 ft, the wall studs shall be increased to 2" × 6" or the studs shall be designed in accordance with accepted engineering practice.

Load-bearing dimension lumber for wall framing must meet the following requirements:

- Identified by a grade mark
- Studs No. 3, standard or stud-grade lumber
  Note: Utility studs are permitted, provided they do not support floors.

The code permits load-bearing studs 11 ft. and 12 ft. high under the following conditions (table 5.5):

- Studs and plates of No. 2 grade lumber
- Maximum live load 20 psf and snow load 30 psf
- Wind exposure category B
- Minimum ½-inch gypsum board on the interior and ⅜-inch wood structural panel sheathing on the exterior
- Minimum 8d (2.5" × 0.131") nails 6 in. O.C. at edges and 12 in. O.C. in field for exterior sheathing
- Exterior panel joints over studs or blocking
- For wind speeds greater than 115 mph, studs attached to plates with connectors rated for 300 lb.

Double top plates are generally required for exterior walls and interior bearing walls. They must meet the following requirements:

- Overlap at corners and intersections with bearing partitions

Table 6.4 Alternate wood bearing wall stud size, height and spacing

Stud Height	Supporting	Stud Spacing	Ultimate Design Wind Speed					
			115 mph Maximum Roof/Floor Span		130 mph Maximum Roof/Floor Span		140 mph Maximum Roof/Floor Span	
			12 ft	24 ft	12 ft	24 ft	12 ft	24 ft
11 ft	Roof Only	12 in.	2x4	2x4	2x4	2x4	2x4	2x4
		16 in.	2x4	2x4	2x4	2x6	2x4	2x6
		24 in.	2x6	2x6	2x6	2x6	2x6	2x6
	Roof and One Floor	12 in.	2x4	2x6	2x4	2x6	2x4	2x6
		16 in.	2x6	2x6	2x6	2x6	2x6	2x6
		24 in.	2x6	2x6	2x6	2x6	2x6	2x6
12 ft	Roof Only	12 in	2x4	2x4	2x4	2x6	2x4	2x6
		16 in.	2x4	2x6	2x6	2x6	2x6	2x6
		24 in.	2x6	2x6	2x6	2x6	2x6	2x6
	Roof and One Floor	12 in	2x4	2x6	2x6	2x6	2x6	2x6
		16 in.	2x6	2x6	2x6	2x6	2x6	2x6
		24 in.	2x6	2x6	2x6	2x6	2x6	DR

DR = Design Required

- End joints offset at least 24 in.

   Note: The code permits a single top plate when studs are in line with joists and rafters, and all plate joints are reinforced with additional connectors.

In dwelling construction, interior and exterior wall studs typically are installed at 16 in. O.C. If the bearing studs are 24 in. O.C., and the joists, trusses, or rafters above them are more than 16 in. O.C., the framing must have one of the following:

- Bearing located within 5 in. of the stud below
- Two 2 × 6 or two 3 × 4 top plates
- A third top plate
- Solid blocking to reinforce double top plate

For interior nonbearing walls, the code permits 2 × 3 studs, 24 in. O.C. or 2 × 4 flat studs, 16 in. O.C.

Drilling and Notching

To preserve the structural integrity of the wall framing, the IRC limits the amount of notching and boring in studs and plates. Notches and bored holes in studs of exterior walls or bearing partitions must meet the following requirements (fig. 6.1):

- Maximum notch 25% of the stud depth
- Maximum hole diameter of 40% of the stud depth
- Edge of hole at least ⅝ in. from edge of stud

top plates

stud

Bored hole
max diameter
40% of stud depth

5/8" min.
to edge

5/8" min.
to edge

Notch must
not exceed
25% of
stud depth

Bored holes shall not be
located in the same cross
section of cut or notch
in stud

If hole is between 40% and 60%
of stud depth, then stud must be
double and no more than two
successive studs are doubled and
so bored

Figure 6.1 Notching and bored hole limitations for exterior walls and bearing walls

Source: International Residential Code for One- and Two-Family Dwellings, 2006. Washington, DC: International Code Council, 2006. p. 132

The code permits drilling of up to 60% diameter holes in studs of exterior walls or bearing partitions provided the studs are doubled, with no more than two successive doubled studs bored.

Notches and bored holes in studs of nonbearing partitions must meet the following requirements (fig. 6.2):

- Maximum notch of 40% of the stud depth
- Maximum hole diameter of 60% of the stud depth
- Edge of hole at least ⅝ in. from edge of stud

Unless wood structural panel sheathing covers the entire side of the wall, top plates of exterior or bearing walls that are drilled or notched more than 50% require reinforcement with a metal strap as follows (fig. 6.3):

- Galvanized metal tie 0.054 in. thick (16 gage) and 1½ in. wide
- Metal tie 6 in. past opening on each side
- Eight joist hanger nails (0.148 in. diameter × 1½ in.) at each side

top plates

Bored hole
max. diameter
60% of stud depth

5/8" min.
to edge

stud

5/8" min.
to edge

Notch must not exceed
40% of stud depth

Bored holes shall not be
located in the same cross
section of cut or notch
in stud

**Figure 6.2 Notching and bored hole limitations for interior
nonbearing walls**

Source: International Residential Code for One- and Two-Family Dwellings, 2006.
Washington, DC: International Code Council, 2006, p. 133

Exterior wall or interior load bearing wall

Plumbing vent
or other pipe

Double
top plate

≥6"

≥6"

Minimum 16 ga.
× 1 1/2"
galvanized steel
plate tie attached
to top plate with
at least 8 nails
0.148" dia. ×
1 1/2" long on
each side
of notch

Studs

Notch greater
than 50% of
width of plate

Approved connector
and joist hanger nail

1 1/2"

0.148"

Figure 6.3 Top plate framing to accommodate piping

Headers

Tables 6.5 and 6.6 provide allowable spans for headers fabricated of dimension lumber and located in an exterior or interior bearing wall. These tables
- Provide the required number of jack studs to support each end
- Consider the overall width of the building and the elements being supported in determining spans
- Include values for ground snow loads of 30, 50, and 70 psf

  Note: The code also prescribes the minimum number of full-height studs at each end of the header based on the header span, wind speed and wind exposure category.

Fireblocking

To stop the spread of fire in concealed spaces of wood frame construction, the IRC requires fireblocking to cut off all concealed draft openings and to form an effective fire barrier between stories and between a top story and the roof space (attic). The following concealed locations require fireblocking:
- Walls at the ceiling and floor levels (by using top and bottom plates in platform framing)
- Walls horizontally at 10 ft. intervals or less (typically provided by studs unless staggered studs are used)

Table 6.5 Girder spans and header spans for exterior bearing walls

Girders and headers supporting	Size	Ground snow load (psf)											
		30				50				70			
		Building width (ft.)											
		24		36		24		36		24		36	
		Span	Jack studs	Span	Jack studs	Span	Jack studs	Span	Jack studs	Span	Jack studs	Span	Jack studs
Roof and ceiling	2-2 × 8	5-9	1	4-10	2	5-0	2	4-2	2	4-5	2	3-9	2
	2-2 × 10	6-10	2	5-9	2	5-11	2	4-11	2	5-3	2	4-5	2
	2-2 × 12	8-1	2	6-10	2	6-11	2	5-10	2	6-2	2	5-2	3
	3-2 × 8	7-3	1	6-1	1	6-3	1	5-3	2	5-6	2	4-8	2
	3-2 × 10	8-7	1	7-3	2	7-4	2	6-2	2	6-7	2	5-6	2
	3-2 × 12	10-1	2	8-6	2	8-8	2	7-4	2	7-9	2	6-6	2
Roof, ceiling, and one center-bearing floor	2-2 × 8	4-10	2	4-1	2	4-5	2	3-9	2	4-1	2	3-6	2
	2-2 × 10	5-8	2	4-10	2	5-3	2	4-5	2	4-10	2	4-1	3
	2-2 × 12	6-8	2	5-8	2	6-2	2	5-3	3	5-8	2	4-10	2
	3-2 × 8	6-0	1	5-1	2	5-6	2	4-8	2	5-1	2	4-4	2
	3-2 × 10	7-2	2	6-1	2	6-7	2	5-7	2	6-1	2	5-2	2
	3-2 × 12	8-5	2	7-2	2	7-8	2	6-7	2	7-1	2	6-1	2

Table 6.5 Girder spans and header spans for exterior bearing walls *(continued)*

	Member	Span	NJ	Span	NJ	Span	NJ	Span	NJ	Span	NJ	Span	NJ
Roof, ceiling and one clear span floor	2-2 × 8	4-3	2	3-7	2	4-0	2	3-4	2	3-9	2	3-2	2
	2-2 × 10	5-0	2	4-2	2	4-9	2	4-0	2	4-5	2	3-9	3
	2-2 × 12	5-11	2	4-11	3	5-7	3	4-8	3	5-3	3	4-5	3
	3-2 × 8	5-3	2	4-5	2	5-0	2	4-2	2	4-8	2	4-0	2
	3-2 × 10	6-3	2	5-3	2	5-11	2	5-0	2	5-7	2	4-8	2
	3-2 × 12	7-5	2	6-2	2	7-0	2	5-10	2	6-7	2	5-6	3
Roof, ceiling and two center-bearing floors	2-2 × 8	4-0	2	3-5	2	3-10	2	3-3	2	3-7	2	3-1	2
	2-2 × 10	4-9	2	4-0	2	4-6	3	3-10	3	4-3	3	3-8	3
	2-2 × 12	5-7	3	4-9	3	5-4	3	4-6	3	5-0	3	4-3	3
	3-2 × 8	5-0	2	4-3	2	4-9	2	4-1	2	4-6	2	3-10	2
	3-2 × 10	5-11	2	5-1	2	5-8	2	4-10	2	5-4	2	4-7	2
	3-2 × 12	7-0	2	5-11	2	6-8	2	5-8	2	6-4	3	5-4	3
Roof, ceiling and two clear-span floors	2-2 × 8	3-3	2	2-8	2	3-3	2	2-8	2	3-2	2	2-8	3
	2-2 × 10	3-10	3	3-2	3	3-10	3	3-2	3	3-9	3	3-2	3
	2-2 × 12	4-6	3	3-9	3	4-6	3	3-9	3	4-5	3	3-9	3
	3-2 × 8	4-0	2	3-5	2	4-0	2	3-5	2	3-11	2	3-4	3
	3-2 × 10	4-9	2	4-0	2	4-9	2	4-0	2	4-8	2	4-0	3
	3-2 × 12	5-8	2	4-9	2	5-8	3	4-9	2	5-6	3	4-8	3

Note: Spans are based on No. 2 Grade Douglas fir-larch, hem-fir, spruce-pine-fir and southern pine.

Table 6.6 Girder spans and header spans for interior bearing walls

Headers and girders supporting	Size	Building width (ft.)					
		12		24		36	
		Span	Jack studs	Span	Jack studs	Span	Jack studs
One floor only	2-2 × 4	4-1	1	2-10	1	2-4	1
	2-2 × 6	6-1	1	4-4	1	3-6	1
	2-2 × 8	7-9	1	5-5	1	4-5	2
	2-2 × 10	9-2	1	6-6	2	5-3	2
	2-2 × 12	10-9	1	7-7	2	6-3	2
	3-2 × 8	9-8	1	6-10	1	5-7	1
	3-2 × 10	11-5	1	8-1	1	6-7	2
	3-2 × 12	13-6	1	9-6	2	7-9	2
	4-2 × 8	11-2	1	7-11	1	6-5	1
	4-2 × 10	13-3	1	9-4	1	7-8	1
	4-2 × 12	15-7	1	11-0	1	9-0	2
Two floors	2-2 × 4	2-7	1	1-11	1	1-7	1
	2-2 × 6	3-11	1	2-11	2	2-5	2
	2-2 × 8	5-0	1	3-8	2	3-1	2
	2-2 × 10	5-11	2	4-4	2	3-7	2
	2-2 × 12	6-11	2	5-2	2	4-3	3
	3-2 × 8	6-3	1	4-7	2	3-10	2
	3-2 × 10	7-5	1	5-6	2	4-6	2
	3-2 × 12	8-8	2	6-5	2	5-4	2
	4-2 × 8	7-2	1	5-4	1	4-5	2
	4-2 × 10	8-6	1	6-4	2	5-3	2
	4-2 × 12	10-1	1	7-5	2	6-2	2

Note: Spans are based on No. 2 Grade lumber of Douglas fir-larch, hem-fir, spruce-pine-fir and southern pine.

- Interconnections between vertical and horizontal spaces, such as those at soffits, drop ceilings, and cove ceilings
- Concealed spaces between stair stringers at the top and bottom of the run
- Openings around vents, pipes, ducts, cables, and wires at ceiling and floor level
- Cornices of two-family dwellings at the separation line

Fireblocking Materials

The code requires an approved material, such as caulking, around vents, pipes, ducts, cables, and wires to resist passage of flame and products of combustion. In other locations, approved fireblocking materials include the following:

- 2 in. nominal lumber
- 2 thicknesses of 1 in. nominal lumber
- $^{23}/_{32}$ in. wood structural panel with joints backed by $^{23}/_{32}$ in. wood structural panel
- ¾ in. particleboard with joints backed by ¾ inch particleboard
- ½ in. gypsum board
- ¼ in. cement-based millboard
- Batts or blankets of mineral wool or glass fiber securely retained in place
- Cellulose insulation installed as tested for the specific application

Foundation Cripple Walls

A cripple wall is a framed wall extending from the top of the foundation to the underside of the floor framing of the first-story-above-*grade* plane. This must meet the following criteria:

- The studs in the cripple wall cannot be smaller than the studs that are above it.
- Unless constructed of solid blocking, an exterior cripple wall with a stud height of less than 14 in. requires wood structural panel sheathing.
- Cripple walls shall be supported on continuous foundations.

Wall Bracing

Wall bracing is necessary to provide resistance to *racking* from lateral loads, primarily wind and seismic forces. The IRC includes various prescriptive methods of isolated panel and diagonal wall bracing, referred to as intermittent bracing methods. In addition to intermittent *braced wall panels* along a *braced wall line,* another, more common, method for compliance with the bracing requirements is continuous sheathing. This method applies wood structural panel or structural fiberboard sheathing to all surfaces along the braced wall line. The code includes several alternatives to both intermittent and continuous methods for narrow wall bracing, typically used at corners or adjacent to large windows or overhead door openings.

Braced Wall Lines

A braced wall line consists of a series of braced wall panels resisting lateral forces in the plane of the wall. The code permits braced wall panels to be offset as much as 4 ft. on either side of the braced wall line (with limitations). For buildings sited in SDC D_0, D_1, or D_2, and townhomes in SDC C, the maximum spacing between braced wall lines typically is 25 ft. Under some circumstances, the code permits an increase to 35 ft. spacing. All buildings located in SDC A or B, and one- and two-family dwellings in SDC C are exempt from the seismic provisions and bracing is based on the design wind speed. In these locations, the spacing between braced wall lines corresponds to the amount of required bracing: greater spacing require requires more bracing. The maximum spacing in this case is 60 ft.

Intermittent Braced Wall Panel Construction Methods
The IRC recognizes 9 methods for constructing intermittent braced wall panels and 3 alternative The most common bracing methods are shown table 6.7. The minimum length of a braced wall panel is typically 4 ft., but the alternatives permit a reduction in this length by increasing panel strength through specific material, connection, and anchorage details. In some cases, the code also permits partial credit for braced wall panels that are less than 4 ft. in actual length in SDC A, B, and C.

A braced wall line must contain the prescribed total length of bracing in feet (table 6.8) and meet the maximum spacing requirements for braced wall panels. The amount and location of bracing is determined by various factors. These include:
- Number of stories
- SDC
- Design wind speed
- Wind exposure category
- Bracing method

Intermittent Braced Wall Panel
Intermittent braced wall panels within a braced wall line must
- Be spaced no more than 20 ft. between panels

- Not be offset out of plane of the braced wall line by more than 4 ft. (8 ft. total out-to-out offset)
- Start within 10 ft. of either end of braced wall line
  Note: Braced wall panels must be located at each end of the braced wall line in seismic design categories D_0, D_1, and D_2 with some exceptions.

Continuous Wood Structural Panel Sheathing

Another way (and typically the most common method) to comply with the wall bracing provisions is to apply wood structural panels to all areas of one side of a braced wall line, including above and below windows. This continuous sheathing method increases the rigidity of the lateral resistance system and allows reduced lengths for full-height braced wall panels. *(See table 6.8 for total required length of bracing in a braced wall line using continuous sheathing and based on a wind speed of 115 mph.)* The minimum length of a braced wall panel is based on the height of the adjacent window or door opening (table 6.9).

When using wood structural panels, continuous sheathing is known as Method CS-WSP. The code also permits continuous structural fiberboard sheathing (Method CS-FSB). The continuous sheathing methods including alternatives are shown in table 6.7.

Table 6.7 Bracing methods

Method	Material	Minimum thickness	Illustration	Connection criteria
LIB	Let-in-bracing	1 × 4 wood or approved metal straps at 45° to 60° angles		Wood: 2 8d common nails or 3 8d (2½" long × 0.113" dia.) nails per stud and top and bottom plates
WSP	Wood structural panel	⅜"		For exterior sheathing see table 6.2 For interior sheathing see table 6.1
SFB	Structural fiberboard sheathing	½" or ²⁵⁄₃₂" for maximum 16" stud spacing		1½" long × 0.12" dia. (for ½" thick sheathing) 1¾" long × 0.12" dia. (for ²⁵⁄₃₂" thick sheathing) galvanized roofing nails; 3" edges, 6" field

ABW	Alternate braced wall	⅜"		See Section R602.10.6.1.
PFH	Portal frame with hold-downs	⅜"		See figure 6.4.
PFG	Portal frame at garage	⁷⁄₁₆"		See figure 6.5.
CS-WSP	Continuously sheathed wood structural panel	⅜"		For exterior sheathing see table 6.2. For interior sheathing see table 6.1.

(continued)

Table 6.7 Bracing methods (*continued*)

Method	Material	Minimum thickness	Illustration	Connection criteria
CS-G	Continuously sheathed wood structural panel adjacent to garage openings	⅜"		For exterior sheathing see table 6.2. For interior sheathing see table 6.1.
CS-PF	Continuously sheathed portal frame	⁷⁄₁₆"		See figure 6.6.
CS-SFB	Continuously sheathed structural fiberboard	½" or ²⁵⁄₃₂" for maximum 16" stud spacing		1½" long × 0.12" dia. (for ½" thick sheathing) 1¾" long × 0.12" dia. (for ²⁵⁄₃₂" thick sheathing) galvanized roofing nails; 3" edges, 6" field

Table 6.8 Bracing requirements based on wind speed

Story Location	Braced wall line spacing (ft.)	Minimum total length (ft.) of braced wall panels required along each braced wall line			
		Method LIB	Method GB	Methods DWB, WSP, SFB, PBS, PCP, HPS, CS-SFB	Methods CS-WSP, CS-G, CS-PF
	10	3.5	3.5	2	2
	20	6.5	6.5	3.5	3.5
	30	9.5	9.5	5.5	4.5
	40	12.5	12.5	7	6
	50	15	15	9	7.5
	60	18	18	10.5	9
	10	7	7	4	3.5
	20	12.5	12.5	7.5	6.5
	30	18	18	10.5	9
	40	23.5	23.5	13.5	11.5
	50	29	29	16.5	14
	60	34.5	34.5	20	17

(continued)

Table 6.8 Bracing requirements based on wind speed *(continued)*

Story Location	Braced wall line spacing (ft.)	Minimum total length (ft.) of braced wall panels required along each braced wall line			
		Method LIB	Method GB	Methods DWB, WSP, SFB, PBS, PCP, HPS, CS-SFB	Methods CS-WSP, CS-G, CS-PF
	10	NP	10	6	5
	20	NP	18.5	11	9
	30	NP	27	15.5	13
	40	NP	35	20	17
	50	NP	43	24.5	21
	60	NP	51	29	25

Bracing amounts are based on the following:
• Ultimate Design Wind Speed 115 mph
• Exposure Category B
• 30 ft mean roof height
• 10 ft eave to ridge height
• 10 ft wall height
• 2 braced wall lines

Table 6.9 Minimum length of braced wall panels for continuous sheathing (methods CS-WSP, CS-SFB)

Adjacent clear opening height (in.)	Wall height (ft.)				
	8	9	10	11	12
64	24	27	30	33	36
68	26	27	30	33	36
72	27	27	30	33	36
76	30	29	30	33	36
80	32	30	30	33	36
84	35	32	32	33	36
88	38	35	33	33	36
92	43	37	35	35	36
96	48	41	38	36	36
100	–	44	40	38	38
104	–	49	43	40	39
108	–	54	46	43	41
112	–	–	50	45	43
116	–	–	55	48	45
120	–	–	60	52	48
124	–	–	–	56	51
128	–	–	–	61	54
132	–	–	–	66	58
136	–	–	–	–	62
140	–	–	–	–	66
144	–	–	–	–	72

Alternate and Portal Frame Braced Wall Panels

The code provides alternative designs, including 3 portal frame methods, for reducing braced wall panel lengths by increasing the strength of the panel through specific material, connection, and anchorage details. The minimum length of the panel for the portal frame methods is based on wall height (table 6.10). The code limits the header height to 10 ft. for these methods but does permit a pony wall above the header to achieve a maximum wall height of 12 ft. Table 6.10 also determines the contributing length of each alternative panel to the required total length of bracing in the wall line.

Method PFH: Portal Frame with Hold-Downs

Method PFH requires hold-down devices for anchorage to the foundation and may be used in all seismic design categories within the scope of the IRC. This is the only narrow wall method that receives full credit as equivalent to a 48 in. braced wall panel. Construction must comply with the details of figure 6.4 as follows:

- Panel length is determined from table 6.10, but must be at least
  - 16 in. for 1-story buildings
  - 24 in. for the first story of 2-story buildings
- Wall height not more than 12 ft.
- Top of header height not more than 10 ft.

Figure 6.4 Method PFH: portal frame with hold-downs

Source: International Residential Code for One- and Two-Family Dwellings, 2015. Washington, DC: International Code Council, 2014, p. 190.

Table 6.10 Minimum length of braced wall panels for portal frame methods

Method		Minimum length (in.)			Contributing length (in.)
		Portal header height			
		8'	9'	10'	
PFH	Supporting roof only	16	16	16	48
	Supporting one story and roof	24	24	24	48
PFG (SDC A, B and C)		24	27	30	1.5 × actual
CS-PF	SDC A, B and C	16	18	20	1.5 × actual
	SDC D_0, D_1, and D_2	16	18	20	actual

Note: Header height is limited to 10 ft. but maximum wall height is 12 ft.

WALL CONSTRUCTION **149**

- Minimum ⅜ in. wood structural panel sheathing on one side
- Full-length header to the first stud of each panel
- Minimum header size 3 in. by 11¼ in. net
- Header strapped to the wall to resist uplift (capacity of strap varies based on opening size, wall height, wind speed, and exposure category)
- Continuous concrete foundation with reinforcement
- One ⅝ in. anchor bolt with a ³⁄₁₆ in. × 2½ in. × 2½ in. plate washer and double bottom plates
- End studs with embedded strap-type hold-down devices rated at 3,500 lb.

Method PFG: Portal Frame at Garage Door Openings in Seismic Design Categories A, B, and C

This method does not require hold-down devices anchored to the foundation but is limited to buildings located in the lower seismic design categories—SDC A, B, and C. This portal frame method also does not get full credit for a 48-in. braced wall panel. The code permits these alternate braced wall panels on either side of garage door openings. Construction must comply with the details of figure 6.5 as follows:

- Panel length must be at least 24 in. and conform to the specifications in table 6.10.
- Wall height, header height, header size, and uplift straps are the same as Method PFH.

Figure 6.5 Method PFG: portal frame at garage door openings in seismic design categories A, B, and C

Source: International Residential Code for One- and Two-Family Dwellings, 2012. Washington, DC: International Code Council, 2011, p. 179.

- ⁷⁄₁₆ in. wood structural panel sheathing one side
- Two ½ in. anchor bolts with ³⁄₁₆ in. by 2½ in. × 2½ in. plate washers

Method CS-PF: Continuously Sheathed Portal Frame

This continuous sheathing method does not require hold-down devices for anchorage to the foundation but generally requires greater panel lengths than Method PFH. This portal frame method also does not get full credit for a 48 in. braced wall panel. Unlike other portal frame construction, Method CS-PF can be supported by wood floor framing. The code permits a maximum of 4 of these portal frame panels in a single braced wall line. Construction must comply with the details of figure 6.6, which are summarized below:

- Panel length is determined from table 6.10, but must be at least 16 in.
- Wall height, header height, header size, and uplift straps are the same as for Method PFH.
- There must be ⁷⁄₁₆ in. wood structural panel sheathing on one side.
- When supported by the foundation, two ½ in. anchor bolts with ³⁄₁₆ in. × 2½ in. × 2½ in. plate washers are required.
- Over a raised wood floor, panels must be connected to floor framing with continuous wood structural panel sheathing or framing anchors rated at 670 lbs.

Fasten top plate header with two rows of 16D sinker nails at 3" O.C. type

Min. 7/16" wood structural panel sheathing

Tension strap per table R602.10.6.4 (on opposite side of sheathing)

If needed panel splice edges shall occur and be attached to common blocking within 24" of wall mid-height. One row of 3" O.C. nailing is required in each panel edge.

Braced wall line continuously sheathed with wood structural panels

Typical portal frame construction

Min. double 2 X 4 post (king and jack stud) number of jack studs per tables R602.5(1) & (2).

Anchor bolts per section R403.1.6

Min. 3" X 11 1/4" net header steel header prohibited

Fasten sheathing to header with 8D common or galvanized box nails in 3" grid pattern as shown

Header to jack-stud strap per table R602.10.6.4 on both sides of opening opposite side of sheathing

Min. double 2x4 framing covered with min. 7/16" thick wood structural panel sheathing with 8D common or galvanized box nails at 3" O.C. in all framing (studs, blocking, and sills) typ.

Min. (2) 1/2" diameter anchor bolts installed per R403.1.6 with 2" X 2" X 3/16" plate washer

Extent of header with double portal frames (two braced wall panels)

Extent of header with single portal frame (one braced wall panel)

2' 18" finished width of opening for single or double portal

Over concrete or masonry block foundation

Pony wall height

10' max. height

12' max total wall height

Figure 6.6 Method CS-PF: continuously sheathed portal frame panel construction

Source: International Residential Code for One- and Two-Family Dwellings, 2012. Washington, DC: International Code Council, 2011, p. 180.

Figure 6.6 Method CS-PF: continuously sheathed portal frame panel construction *(continued)*

Source: International Residential Code for One- and Two-Family Dwellings, 2012. Washington, DC: International Code Council, 2011, p. 180.

Simplified Wall Bracing

The IRC offers a simplified method of wall bracing that can be used in most parts of the country without requiring complex calculations or adjustment factors. This method is limited to buildings that meet all of the following requirements:

- Maximum three stories above a concrete or masonry foundation or basement wall
- No floor cantilever more than 24 in.
- Maximum wall height of 10 ft.
- Maximum roof eave-to-ridge height of 15 ft.
- Minimum ½ in. gypsum board on the interior side of walls
- Maximum wind speed 130 mph and Exposure Category B or C
- SDC A, B, or C for detached one- and two-family dwellings
- SDC A or B for townhomes
- No cripple walls permitted in three-story buildings

Circumscribed Rectangle

When a rectangle is drawn around the building including the attached garage but excluding decks, open porches, and carports, the following requirements apply (fig. 6.7):

- Maximum 60 ft. dimension on any side
- Maximum ratio of long side to short side of 3:1

Figure 6.7 Simple bracing

Bracing Units

For simplified wall bracing, each section of bracing is called a bracing unit rather than a braced wall panel. Bracing units must

- Be constructed with minimum ⅜ in. wood structural panels or ½ in. structural fiberboard sheathing
- Be at least 3 ft. long when continuous sheathing is of the same material
- Be at least 4 ft. long for intermittent bracing units
- Have no more than 20 ft. of spacing from edge to edge
- Not be inset more than 12 ft. from the corner
- Have at least 1 bracing unit for wall segments longer than 8 ft.

The minimum number of bracing units is determined from table 6.11.

Narrow panels

The code permits using the portal frame construction methods CS-PF, PFH, and PFG as discussed under the conventional wall bracing provisions, in addition to Method CS-G, (continuously sheathed wood structural panel adjacent to garage openings). The code requires continuous wood structural panel sheathing on all walls and assigns partial credit in

Table 6.11 Minimum number of bracing units on each side of the circumscribed rectangle

Ultimate design wind Speed (mph)	Story level	Eave-to-ridge height (ft.)	Minimum number of bracing units on each long side — Length of short side (ft.)						Minimum number of bracing units on each short side — Length of long side (ft.)					
			10	20	30	40	50	60	10	20	30	40	50	60
115	⌂⌂⌂	10	1	2	2	2	3	3	1	2	2	2	3	3
	⌂⌂		2	3	3	4	5	6	2	3	3	4	5	6
	⌂		2	3	4	6	7	8	2	3	4	6	7	8
	⌂⌂⌂	15	1	2	3	3	4	4	1	2	3	3	4	4
	⌂⌂		2	3	4	5	6	7	2	3	4	5	6	7
	⌂		2	4	5	6	7	9	2	4	5	6	7	9

Table 6.11 Minimum number of bracing units on each side of the circumscribed rectangle *(continued)*

Ultimate design wind Speed (mph)	Story level	Eave-to-ridge height (ft.)	Minimum number of bracing units on each long side — Length of short side (ft.)						Minimum number of bracing units on each short side — Length of long side (ft.)					
			10	20	30	40	50	60	10	20	30	40	50	60
130	(building icon)	10	1	2	2	3	3	4	1	2	2	3	3	4
	(building icon)		2	3	4	5	6	7	2	3	4	5	6	7
	(building icon)		2	4	5	7	8	10	2	4	5	7	8	10
	(building icon)	15	2	3	3	4	4	6	2	3	3	4	4	6
	(building icon)		3	4	6	7	8	10	3	4	6	7	8	10
	(building icon)		3	6	7	10	11	13	3	6	7	10	11	13

Note: For Exposure Category C, multiply bracing units by a factor of 1.20 for a one-story building, 1.30 for a two-story building and 1.40 for a three-story building.

number of bracing units for these narrow panel methods as follows:

- CSG = 0.5 bracing unit
- CS-PF = 0.75 bracing unit
- PFG = 0.75 bracing unit
- PFH = 1.0 bracing unit

  Note: Method CS-G is only permitted on one-story garages.

Steel Wall Framing

The code contains prescriptive requirements for cold-formed steel wall framing applicable to buildings not greater than 40 × 60 ft. and up to 3 stories high. Use of these code provisions is further limited to sites with a wind speed less than 140 mph and a ground snow load of 70 psf.

Exterior Windows and Doors

Windows and doors located in exterior walls must be installed, anchored, and flashed according to the manufacturer's written installation instructions. The code requires the manufacturer to provide written installation instructions for each window or door. Garage doors require a permanent label provided by the manufacturer. The label identifies the positive and negative design wind pressure rating and the applicable test standard among other requirements.

Structural Insulated Panel (SIP) Wall Construction

The IRC contains prescriptive requirements for SIP wall construction that applies to buildings that do not exceed the following criteria:

- 60 ft. long
- 40 ft. wide
- 2 stories high
- 10 ft. wall height
- SDC A, B, and C
- 70 psf ground snow load
- 155 mph ultimate design wind speed in Exposure B or 140 mph in Exposure C

The code provides tabular values for the minimum thickness of SIP wall construction based on
- Building width
- Roof or story and roof being supported
- Wall height
- Snow load
- Wind speed
- Wind exposure category

7

Wall Covering

This chapter addresses the design and installation of interior and exterior wall coverings. Interior gypsum board (drywall) and plaster must meet minimum thicknesses. The code includes minimum fastener requirements as well. Exterior surfaces must be protected from the weather with appropriate water-resistive barriers, flashing, and finish surfaces such as siding, veneer, or plaster (stucco).

Interior Wall Coverings

Interior wall coverings shall not be installed until the area is protected from the weather. The code contains prescriptive installation requirements for gypsum board (drywall). Minimum fastening and thickness requirements are dependent on the spacing of the framing members and the location and intended application of the gypsum board. The code also contains tables for minimum thicknesses of plaster coats, but refers installers to applicable ASTM standards for material and installation details.

Vapor Retarders

A Class I or Class II vapor retarder is required on the interior side of above-grade frame walls in Climate Zones 5, 6, 7, 8, and Marine 4. Sheet polyethylene is an example of a Class I vapor retarder. Kraft-faced fiberglass batt insulation is an example of a Class II vapor retarder.

Gypsum Board Application

Gypsum board can be installed perpendicular or parallel to framing members in accordance with table 7.1, with the following exceptions:

- ⅜ in. must be installed perpendicular to ceiling framing members and is not permitted on ceilings receiving water-based textures or supporting insulation.
- ½ in. must be applied perpendicular to ceiling members spaced 16 in. O.C. when ceilings will receive water-based texture finishes (unless high-strength gypsum board is used).
- ⅝ in. Type X installed on ceilings of garages to separate them from habitable rooms located above the garage must be perpendicular to the framing members.

Table 7.1 Minimum thickness and application of gypsum board

Thickness of gypsum board (in.)	Application	Orientation of gypsum board to framing	Maximum spacing of framing members (in. O.C.)	Maximum spacing of fasteners (in.)		Size of nails for application to wood framing
				Nails	Screws	
			Application without adhesive			
3/8	Ceiling	Perpendicular	16	7	12	13 gauge, 1¼" long, 19/64" head; 0.098" diameter, 1¼" long ring shank, or 4d cooler nail, 0.080" diameter, 1⅜" long, 7/32" head
	Wall	Either direction	16	8	16	
1/2	Ceiling	Either direction	16	7	12	13 gauge, 1⅜" long, 19/64" head; 0.098" diameter, 1¼" long ring shank, 5d cooler nail, 0.086"
	Ceiling	Perpendicular	24	7	12	
	Wall	Either direction	24	8	12	diameter, 1⅝" long, 15/64" head; or gypsum board nail, 0.086" diameter,
	Wall	Either direction	16	8	16	1⅝" long, 9/32" head

(continued)

Table 7.1 Minimum thickness and application of gypsum board *(continued)*

Thickness of gypsum board (in.)	Application	Orientation of gypsum board to framing	Maximum spacing of framing members (in. O.C.)	Maximum spacing of fasteners (in.)		Size of nails for application to wood framing
				Nails	Screws	
			Application without adhesive (continued)			
	Ceiling	Either direction	16	7	12	13 gauge, 1⅜" long, ¹⁹⁄₆₄" head; 0.098" diameter, 1⅜" long ring shank, 6d cooler nail,
	Ceiling	Perpendicular	24	7	12	
	Wall	Either direction	24	8	12	0.092" diameter, 1⅞" long, ¼"
	Wall	Either direction	16	8	16	head; or gypsum board nail, 0.0915" diameter, 1⅞" long, ¹⁹⁄₆₄" head
⅝	Type X at garage ceiling beneath habitable rooms	Perpendicular	24	6	6	1⅞ long 0.099" diameter galvanized nails or equivalent drywall screws. Screws shall comply with Section R702.3.5.1

			Application with adhesive			
3/8	Ceiling	Perpendicular	16	16	16	Same as above for 3/8" gypsum board
	Wall	Either direction	16	16	24	
1/2 or 5/8	Ceiling	Either direction	16	16	16	Same as above for 1/2" and 5/8" gypsum board, respectively
	Ceiling	Perpendicular	24	12	16	
	Wall	Either direction	24	16	16	
Two 3/8 layers	Ceiling	Perpendicular	16	16	16	Base ply nailed as above for 1/2" gypsum board; face ply installed with adhesive
	Wall	Either direction	24	24	24	

Note: See specific limitations on ceiling applications related to support of insulation, water-based textures, and fire resistance.

Table 7.1 also includes nail and screw fastening requirements. The type of screws to be used depends on the material the gypsum board will be attached to as follows:

- Wood—type W or S screws that penetrate wood at least ⅝ in.
- Cold-formed steel framing—approved screws that comply with the referenced standards and that penetrate steel at least ⅜ in.
- *Structural insulated panels*—approved screws that penetrate wood structural panel sheathing at least ⁷⁄₁₆ in.

Water-Resistant Gypsum Backing Board

Cut or exposed edges must be sealed. Water-resistant gypsum backing board is permitted on ceilings where framing spacing does not exceed 12 in. O.C. for ½ in., or 16 in. O.C. for ⅝ in. It is not allowed

- Over a vapor retarder in a shower or tub compartment
- In areas with direct exposure to water or that are subject to continuous high humidity
- As a backer for ceramic wall tile in tub and shower areas

Ceramic Tile

Ceramic tile surfaces must be installed according the
ANSI standards referenced. The code also requires
one of the following materials as a backer for ceramic
wall tile in tub and shower areas:

■ Fiber cement
■ Fiber-mat-reinforced cement
■ Glass mat gypsum backer
■ Fiber-reinforced gypsum backer

Exterior Wall Coverings

Table 7.2 lists siding and veneer attachment and
installation requirements. Wall coverings must
provide a weather-resistant exterior wall envelope
including the following:

■ Flashings at openings, penetrations, and intersections of materials
■ Water-resistant barrier behind exterior veneer
or siding
■ Means of draining water that enters the exterior
wall assembly to the exterior
■ Protection against condensation in the assembly

Alternative assemblies are permitted if they have been
proven to resist wind-driven rain. Additional covering
is not required over masonry and concrete walls that
are properly flashed.

Table 7.2 Siding minimum attachment and minimum thickness

Siding material		Nominal thickness (in.)	Joint treatment	Type of supports for the siding material and fasteners						
				Wood or wood structural panel sheathing into stud	Fiberboard sheathing into stud	Gypsum sheathing into stud	Foam plastic sheathing into stud	Direct to studs	Number or spacing of fasteners
Anchored veneer: brick, concrete, masonry or stone		2	Per Section R703.8	Per Section R703.8					
Adhered veneer: concrete, stone or masonry		—	Per Section R703.12	Per Section R703.12					
Fiber-cement siding	Panel siding	⁵⁄₁₆	Per Section R703.10.1	6d common (2" × 0.113")	6d common (2" × 0.113")	6d common (2" × 0.113")	6d common (2" × 0.113")	4d common (1½" × 0.099")	6" panel edges 12" inter. sup.
	Lap siding	⁵⁄₁₆	Per Section R703.10.2	6d common (2" × 0.113")	6d common (2" × 0.113")	6d common (2" × 0.113")	6d common (2" × 0.113")	6d common (2" × 0.113") or 11 gage roofing nail	—

Hardboard panel siding		7/16	—	0.120" nail (shank) with 0.225" head	0.120" nail (shank) with 0.225" head	0.120" nail (shank) with 0.225" head	0.120" nail (shank) with 0.225" head	6" panel edges 12" inter. sup.
Hardboard lap siding		7/16	—	0.099" nail (shank) with 0.240" head	0.099" nail (shank) with 0.240" head	0.099" nail (shank) with 0.240" head	0.099" nail (shank) with 0.240" head	Same as stud spacing 2 per bearing
Horizontal aluminum	Without insulation	0.019	Lap	Siding nail 1½" × 0.120"	Siding nail 2" × 0.120"	Siding nail 2" × 0.120"	Siding nail 1½" × 0.120"	Same as stud spacing
	Without insulation	0.024	Lap	Siding nail 1½" × 0.120"	Siding nail 2" × 0.120"	Siding nail 2" × 0.120"	Siding nailh 1½" × 0.120"	
	With insulation	0.019	Lap	Siding nail 1½" × 0.120"	Siding nail 2½" × 0.120"	Siding nail 2½" × 0.120"	Siding nailh 1½" × 0.120"	Siding nail 1½" × 0.120"
Insulated vinyl siding		0.035 (vinyl siding layer only)	Lap	0.120 nail (shank) with a 0.313 head or 16 gauge crown	0.120 nail (shank) with a 0.313 head or 16 gauge crown	0.120 nail (shank) with a 0.313 head per Section R703.11.2	Not allowed	16 in. on center or specified by manufacturer instructions, test report or other sections of the code

(continued)

Table 7.2 Siding minimum attachment and minimum thickness *(continued)*

Siding material	Nominal thickness (in.)	Joint treatment	Type of supports for the siding material and fasteners						Number or spacing of fasteners
			Wood or wood structural panel sheathing into stud	Fiberboard sheathing into stud	Gypsum sheathing into stud	Foam plastic sheathing into stud	Direct to studs		
Particleboard panels	⅜	–	6d box nail (2" × 0.099")	6d box nail (2" × 0.099")	6d box nail (2" × 0.099")	6d box nail (2" × 0.099")	Not allowed		6" panel edges 12" inter. sup.
	½	–	6d box nail (2" × 0.099")	6d box nail (2" × 0.099")	6d box nail (2" × 0.099")	6d box nail (2" × 0.099")	6d box nail (2" × 0.099")		
	⅝	–	6d box nail (2" × 0.099")	8d box nail (2½" × 0.113")	8d box nail (2½" × 0.113")	6d box nail (2" × 0.099")	6d box nail (2" × 0.099")		
Polypropylene siding	Not applicable	Lap	Section 703.14.1	Section 703.14.1	Section 703.14.1	Section 703.14.1	Not allowed		As specified by the manufacturer instructions, test report or other sections of this code

Material	Type	Thickness	Joint	Fastener A	Fastener B	Fastener C	Fastener D	Fastener E	Fastener spacing
Steel		29 ga.	Lap	Siding nail (1¾" × 0.113") Staple-1¾"	Siding nail (2¾" × 0.113") Staple-2½"	Siding nail (2½" × 0.113") Staple-2¼"	Siding nail (1⅞" × 0.113") Staple-1¾"	Not allowed	Same as stud spacing
Vinyl siding		0.035	Lap	0.120" nail (shank) with a 0.313" head or 16 gauge staple with ⅜–1½" crown	0.120" nail (shank) with a 0.313" head or 16 gauge staple with ⅜–1½" crown	0.120" nail (shank) with a 0.313" head or 16 gauge staple with ⅜–1½" crown	0.120 nail (shank) with a 0.313 head per Section R703.11.2	Not allowed	16 in. on center or specified by the manufacturer instructions or test report
Wood siding	Wood rustic drop	⅜ Min	Lap	6d box or siding nail (2" × 0.099")	6d box or siding nail (2" × 0.099")	6d box or siding nail (2" × 0.099")	6d box or siding nail (2" × 0.099")	8d box or siding nail (2½" × 0.113") Staple-2"	Face nailing up to 6" widths, 1 nail per bearing; 8" widths and over, 2 nails per bearing
	Shiplap	19/32 Average	Lap						
	Bevel	7/16	Lap						
	Butt tip	3/16	Lap						
Wood structural panel ANSI/APA PRP-210 siding (exterior grade)		3/8 –1/2	—	2" × 0.099" siding nail	2½" × 0.113" siding nail	2½" × 0.115" siding nail	2½" × 0.115" siding nail	2" × 0.099" siding nail	6" panel edges 12" inter. sup.
Wood structural panel lap siding		3/8 –1/2	—	2" × 0.099" siding nail	2½" × 0.113" siding nail	2½" × 0.115" siding nail	2½" × 0.115" siding nail	2" × 0.099" siding nail	8" along bottom edge

Water-Resistive Barrier

One layer of No. 15 asphalt felt or other approved water-resistive barrier, such as an approved house wrap, is required over studs or sheathing of all exterior walls. No. 15 asphalt felt must be applied as follows:

- Horizontally
- Upper layers lapped over the lower layers at least 2 in.
- Vertical joints lapped at least 6 in.

Note: House wrap must be installed in accordance with the manufacturer's instructions.

Flashing Requirements Applicable to All Exterior Wall Coverings

To prevent water entering behind exterior wall coverings and penetrating the wall assembly, the code requires corrosion-resistant flashing at the following locations:

- Exterior window and door openings
- The intersection of masonry construction with frame or stucco walls
- Under and at the ends of masonry, wood, or metal copings and sills
- Continuously above all projecting wood trim
- Where exterior porches, decks, or stairs attach to a wall or floor
- At wall and roof intersections

Exterior Insulation and Finish Systems (EIFS)

Installation of EIFS must comply with the referenced ASTM standards and the manufacturer's instructions to provide the code-prescribed weather-resistant exterior envelope. The code permits EIFS without drainage over masonry and concrete construction only. For all other EIFS installations, including those over wood-frame construction, the IRC requires EIFS with drainage. To further protect the integrity of the system, the code also stipulates the following:

- No face nailing of decorative trim through EIFS
- Termination at least 6 in. above the finished ground level

Siding

The code includes installation requirements for both panel and horizontal lapped siding made of wood, hardboard, wood structural panel, fiber cement, and vinyl. Installation must follow the manufacturer's requirements and the code provisions.

Wood, Hardboard, and Wood Structural Panel Siding

For panel siding, horizontal joints must occur over solid blocking or wood structural panel sheathing and comply with one of the following:

- Lapped at least 1 in.
- Shiplapped
- Flashed with z flashing

Vertical joints must occur over framing members or wood structural panel sheathing and be either shiplapped or covered with a batten.

For horizontal lap siding, laps must comply with the manufacturer's recommendations or, if there are no recommendations, the lap must be at least 1 in. (or ½ in. if *rabbeted*). End joints must be made weather tight with one of the following methods:

- Caulked
- Covered with a batten
- Sealed and installed over a strip of flashing

Fiber Cement Siding

Fiber cement siding is manufactured of portland cement, sand, wood fiber, and specialty additives. For vertical panel applications, vertical and horizontal joints must

- Occur over framing members
- Be sealed, covered with battens or flashed

For horizontal lap siding applications, the code requires at least a 1¼ in. lap. End joints require one of the following treatments:

- Sealed with caulking
- Covered with an H-section joint cover
- Located over a strip of flashing
- Tongue and groove

Vinyl Siding

The IRC references the manufacturer's instructions for installing vinyl siding, soffit, and accessories. Each soffit panel must be fastened to framing or supporting components such as:

- Nailing strips
- Fascia or sub-fascia

When vinyl siding is installed over foam plastic sheathing that is not backed with structural sheathing, the code sets specific criteria for resisting design wind pressure. For locations with a wind speed not greater than 115 mph that fall within Exposure Category B, the minimum fastener requirements are:

- 1¼ in. penetration into wood framing
- 0.120-in. diameter nail
- 0.313-in. diameter head
- Nails spaced 16 in. O.C.

Vinyl siding installation in locations with a greater wind speed or exposure category must be

- Adjusted according to the design wind pressures or
- Comply with the manufacturer's specifications for the applicable wind pressure rating

Wood Shakes and Shingles

As with other exterior wall coverings, wood shakes and shingles require an approved water-resistive barrier, such as felt or house wrap. Other installation requirements are as follows:

- Shakes and shingles are attached to wood-based sheathing or furring strips.
- Spacing between shingles is ⅛ to ¼ in.
- Spacing between shakes is ⅜ to ½ in.
- Each shingle or shake requires two corrosion-resistant box nails.
- Bottom courses must be doubled.
- The offset of joints in adjacent courses must be at least 1½ in.

Stone and Masonry Veneer

In general, stone and masonry veneers are limited to the first story and are not greater than 5 in. thick, according to the prescriptive provisions of the IRC. Exceptions allow veneers up to 3 stories and 30 ft. above noncombustible foundations (plus 8 ft. for gables) for wood frame construction depending on the SDC, the nominal thickness and weight of the veneer, and the use of the building (tables 7.3 and 7.4).

Table 7.3 Stone or masonry veneer limitations and requirements, wood or steel framing, seismic design categories A, B, and C

Seismic design category	Wood or steel framing	Number of stories	Maximum height of veneer above noncombustible foundation (ft.)	Maximum nominal thickness of veneer (in.)	Maximum weight of veneer (psf)
A, B, or C	Steel	1 or 2	30	5	50
	Wood	1, 2, or 3	30	5	50

Note: An additional 8 ft. of height is permitted for gable end walls.

Table 7.4 Stone or masonry veneer limitations and requirements, one- and two-family detached dwellings, wood framing, seismic design categories D_0, D_1, and D_2

Seismic design category	Number of wood framed stories	Maximum height of veneer above noncombustible foundation (ft.)	Maximum nominal thickness of veneer (in.)	Maximum weight of veneer (psf)
D_0	1 or 2	20	4	40
	3	30	4	40
D_1	1 or 2	20	4	40
	3	20	4	40
D_2	1 or 2	20	3	30

Note: An additional 8 ft. of height is permitted for gable end walls.

Support

Masonry veneer typically is supported by a continuous concrete or masonry foundation. In seismic design categories A, B, and C, the code permits the following methods of support:

- Directly on wood frame or steel frame construction when designed to limit deflection to $\frac{1}{600}$ of the span of the supporting members
- On a steel angle support measuring at least 6 × 4 × $\frac{5}{16}$ in. and attached to wall construction as follows:
  - Long leg of angle placed vertically
  - Attached to double 2 × 4 studs with two $\frac{7}{16}$ × 4 in. lag screws at 16 in. O.C.
  - Bearing of at least $\frac{2}{3}$ of veneer width
  - Flashing and weep holes above the angle
  - Maximum 12 ft., 8 in. veneer height

Lintels

To support veneer above openings, the code requires noncombustible lintels with a bearing of at least 4 in. at each end. Table 7.5 provides spans for both steel angle and reinforced masonry lintels based on the number of stories above the lintel. Steel angle lintels must be installed with the long leg of the angle situated vertically. They must be protected from corrosion in one of the following ways:

Table 7.5 Allowable spans for lintels supporting masonry veneer

Size of steel angle (in.)	No story above (ft.-in.)	One story above (ft.-in.)	Two stories above (ft.-in.)	No. of ½″ or equivalent reinforcing bars
3 × 3 × ¼	6-0	4-6	3-0	1
4 × 3 × ¼	8-0	6-0	4-6	1
5 × 3½ × 5⁄16	10-0	8-0	6-0	2
6 × 3½ × 5⁄16	14-0	9-6	7-0	2
2–6 × 3½ × 5⁄16	20-0	12-0	9-6	4

Note: Long leg of the angle shall be placed in a vertical position.

Depth of reinforced lintels shall not be less than 8 in., and all cells of hollow masonry lintels shall be grouted solid.

Reinforcing bars shall extend not less than 8 in. into the support.

Steel members indicated are adequate typical examples; other steel members meeting structural design requirements may be used.

- Shop-coated with rust-inhibitive paint
- Made of corrosion-resistant steel
- Treated with corrosion-resistant coating

Veneer Anchored with Corrosion-Resistant Metal Ties

The IRC prescribes the type, size, and location of corrosion-resistant metal ties to anchor the veneer to the supporting structure. The gage or stiffness of the tie depends on the amount of air space behind the veneer. Other requirements are as follows:

- Maximum tie spacing 32 in. O.C. horizontally and 24 in. O.C. vertically
- Maximum supported area 2.67 sq. ft. per tie
- Additional ties around openings
- Minimum 1½ in. tie embedment
- Minimum ⅝ in. mortar cover to outside face

Note: In SDC D_0, D_1, D_2, or for townhomes in SDC C each tie shall support no more than 2 sq. ft. of wall area.

Veneer Details

To provide an adequate weather-resistant exterior wall envelope, exterior stone and masonry veneer require an air space and water-resistant components to prevent moisture from entering into the wall assembly (figs. 7.1a and 7.1b). The IRC requires the following:

- An approved water-resistant barrier over the wall sheathing and behind the veneer
- An air space of nominal 1 in. between the veneer and the sheathing when corrugated sheet metal ties are used
- Greater air spaces up to 6⅝ in. require heavier ties
- Flashing below the first course of masonry veneer above grade and above other points of support
- Weep holes of at least 3/16 in. diameter and spaced no more than 33 in. O.C. immediately above the flashing

Figure 7.1a Masonry veneer details at foundation and sill

Source: International Residential Code for One- and Two-Family Dwellings, 2006. Washington, DC: International Code Council Inc., 2006, p. 236.

Figure 7.1b Masonry veneer details at soffit and lintel (*continued*)

Source: International Residential Code for One- and Two-Family Dwellings, 2006. Washington, DC: International Code Council Inc., 2006, p. 237.

8

Roof Framing

This chapter addresses conventional wood-frame roof-ceiling construction. Maximum ceiling joist spans are for attics without, or with limited, storage (tables 8.1–8.2). (Habitable attics and attics with fixed stair access require joists sized as floor joists.) The prescriptive tables setting maximum spans for rafters are based on the snow load of the geographic area and whether the rafter also supports a ceiling (tables 8.3–8.8). The tables assume a roof live load of 20 psf for regions without snow loads. This chapter also covers attic access and ventilation.

Wood Roof Framing Details

The conventional roof framing provisions in the code apply to roofs with a slope of not less than 3:12. The code prescribes the following framing details:

- Typically rafters are framed opposite each other to a ridge board, but gusset plate ties also are permitted.

Table 8.1 Ceiling joist spans for common lumber species, No. 2 grade

(uninhabitable attics without storage, live load = 10 psf, L/240)

Ceiling joist spacing (in.)	Species	Dead load = 5 psf			
		2 × 4	2 × 6	2 × 8	2 × 10
		Maximum ceiling joist spans			
		(ft.-in.)	(ft.-in.)	(ft.-in.)	(ft.-in.)
12	Douglas fir-larch	12-5	19-6	25-8	> 26-0
	Hem-fir	11-7	18-2	24-0	> 26-0
	Southern pine	11-10	18-8	24-7	> 26-0
	Spruce-pine-fir	11-10	18-8	24-7	> 26-0
16	Douglas fir-larch	11-3	17-8	23-4	> 26-0
	Hem-fir	10-6	16-6	21-9	> 26-0
	Southern pine	10-9	16-11	21-7	25-7
	Spruce-pine-fir	10-9	16-11	22-4	> 26-0
19.2	Douglas fir-larch	10-7	16-8	21-4	26-0
	Hem-fir	9-11	15-7	20-6	25-3
	Southern pine	10-2	15-7	19-8	23-5
	Spruce-pine-fir	10-2	15-11	21-0	25-8
24	Douglas fir-larch	9-10	15-0	19-1	23-3
	Hem-fir	9-2	14-5	18-6	22-7
	Southern pine	9-3	13-11	17-7	20-11
	Spruce-pine-fir	9-5	14-9	18-9	22-11

Table 8.2 Ceiling joist spans for common lumber species, No. 2 grade

(uninhabitable attics with limited storage, live load = 20 psf, L/240)

Ceiling joist spacing (in.)	Species	Dead load = 10 psf			
		2 × 4	2 × 6	2 × 8	2 × 10
		Maximum ceiling joist spans			
		(ft.-in.)	(ft.-in.)	(ft.-in.)	(ft.-in.)
12	Douglas fir-larch	9-10	15-0	19-1	23-3
	Hem-fir	9-2	14-5	18-6	22-7
	Southern pine	9-3	13-11	17-7	20-11
	Spruce-pine-fir	9-5	14-9	18-9	22-11
16	Douglas fir-larch	8-11	13-0	16-6	20-2
	Hem-fir	8-4	12-8	16-0	19-7
	Southern pine	8-0	12-0	15-3	18-1
	Spruce-pine-fir	8-7	12-10	16-3	19-10
19.2	Douglas fir-larch	8-2	11-11	15-1	18-5
	Hem-fir	7-10	11-7	14-8	17-10
	Southern pine	7-4	11-0	13-11	16-6
	Spruce-pine-fir	8-0	11-9	14-10	18-2
24	Douglas fir-larch	7-3	10-8	13-6	16-5
	Hem-fir	7-1	10-4	13-1	16-0
	Southern pine	6-7	9-10	12-6	14-9
	Spruce-pine-fir	7-2	10-6	13-3	16-3

Table 8.3 Rafter spans for common lumber species, No. 2 grade

(roof live load = 20 psf, ceiling not attached to rafters, L/180, dead load = 10 psf)

Rafter spacing (in.)	Species	Dead load = 10 psf				
		2 × 4	2 × 6	2 × 8	2 × 10	2 × 12
		Maximum rafter spans				
		(ft.-in.)	(ft.-in.)	(ft.-in.)	(ft.-in.)	(ft.-in.)
12	Douglas fir-larch	10-10	16-10	21-4	26-0	> 26-0
	Hem-fir	10-1	15-11	20-8	25-3	> 26-0
	Southern pine	10-4	15-7	19-8	23-5	> 26-0
	Spruce-pine-fir	10-4	16-3	21-0	25-8	> 26-0
16	Douglas fir-larch	9-10	14-7	18-5	22-6	26-0
	Hem-fir	9-2	14-2	17-11	21-11	25-5
	Southern pine	9-0	13-6	17-1	20-3	23-10
	Spruce-pine-fir	9-5	14-4	18-2	22-3	25-9
19.2	Douglas fir-larch	9-1	13-3	16-10	20-7	23-10
	Hem-fir	8-8	12-11	16-4	20-0	23-2
	Southern pine	8-2	12-3	15-7	18-6	21-9
	Spruce-pine-fir	8-10	13-1	16-7	20-3	23-6
24	Douglas fir-larch	8-2	11-11	15-1	18-5	21-4
	Hem-fir	7-11	11-7	14-8	17-10	20-9
	Southern pine	7-4	11-0	10-11	16-6	19-6
	Spruce-pine-fir	8-0	11-9	14-10	18-2	21-0

Table 8.4 Rafter spans for common lumber species, No. 2 grade

(roof live load = 20 psf, ceiling attached to rafters, L/240, dead load = 10 psf)

Rafter spacing (in.)	Species	Dead load = 10 psf				
		2 × 4	2 × 6	2 × 8	2 × 10	2 × 12
		Maximum rafter spans				
		(ft.-in.)	(ft.-in.)	(ft.-in.)	(ft.-in.)	(ft.-in.)
12	Douglas fir-larch	9-10	15-6	20-5	26-0	> 26-0
	Hem-fir	9-2	14-5	19-0	24-3	> 26-0
	Southern pine	9-5	14-9	19-6	23-5	> 26-0
	Spruce-pine-fir	9-5	14-9	19-6	24-10	> 26-0
16	Douglas fir-larch	8-11	14-1	18-5	22-6	26-0
	Hem-fir	8-4	13-1	17-3	21-11	25-5
	Southern pine	8-7	13-5	17-1	20-3	23-10
	Spruce-pine-fir	8-7	13-5	17-9	22-3	25-9
19.2	Douglas fir-larch	8-5	13-3	16-10	20-7	23-10
	Hem-fir	7-10	12-4	16-3	20-0	23-2
	Southern pine	8-1	12-3	15-7	18-6	21-9
	Spruce-pine-fir	8-1	12-8	16-7	20-3	23-6
24	Douglas fir-larch	7-10	11-11	15-1	18-5	21-4
	Hem-fir	7-3	11-5	14-8	17-10	20-9
	Southern pine	7-4	11-0	13-11	16-6	19-6
	Spruce-pine-fir	7-6	11-9	14-10	18-2	21-0

Table 8.5 Rafter spans for common lumber species, No. 2 grade

(ground snow load = 30 psf, ceiling not attached to rafters, L/180, dead load = 10 psf)

Rafter spacing (in.)	Species	Dead Load = 10 psf				
		2 × 4	2 × 6	2 × 8	2 × 10	2 × 12
		Maximum rafter spans				
		(ft.-in.)	(ft.-in.)	(ft.-in.)	(ft.-in.)	(ft.-in.)
12	Douglas fir-larch	9-6	14-0	17-8	21-7	25-1
	Hem-fir	8-10	13-7	17-2	21-0	24-4
	Southern pine	8-7	12-11	16-4	19-5	22-10
	Spruce-pine-fir	9-1	13-9	17-5	21-4	24-8
16	Douglas fir-larch	8-3	12-1	15-4	18-9	21-8
	Hem-fir	8-0	11-9	14-11	18-2	21-1
	Southern pine	7-6	11-2	14-2	16-10	19-10
	Spruce-pine-fir	8-2	11-11	15-1	18-5	21-5
19.2	Douglas fir-larch	7-7	11-0	14-0	17-1	19-10
	Hem-fir	7-4	10-9	13-7	16-7	19-3
	Southern pine	6-10	10-2	12-11	15-4	18-1
	Spruce-pine-fir	7-5	10-11	13-9	16-10	19-6
24	Douglas fir-larch	6-9	9-10	12-6	15-3	17-9
	Hem-fir	6-7	9-7	12-2	14-10	17-3
	Southern pine	6-1	9-2	11-7	13-9	16-2
	Spruce-pine-fir	6-8	9-9	12-4	15-1	17-6

Table 8.6 Rafter spans for common lumber species, No. 2 grade
(ground snow load = 50 psf, ceiling not attached to rafters, L/180,
dead load = 10 psf)

Rafter spacing (in.)	Species	Dead load = 10 psf				
		2 × 4	2 × 6	2 × 8	2 × 10	2 × 12
		Maximum rafter spans				
		(ft.-in.)	(ft.-in.)	(ft.-in.)	(ft.-in.)	(ft.-in.)
12	Douglas fir-larch	7-10	11-5	14-5	17-8	20-5
	Hem-fir	7-5	11-1	14-0	17-2	19-11
	Southern pine	7-0	10-6	13-4	15-10	18-8
	Spruce-pine-fir	7-8	11-3	14-3	17-5	15-2
16	Douglas fir-larch	6-9	9-10	12-6	15-3	17-9
	Hem-fir	6-7	9-7	12-2	14-10	17-3
	Southern pine	6-1	9-2	11-7	13-9	16-2
	Spruce-pine-fir	6-8	9-9	12-4	15-1	17-6
19.2	Douglas fir-larch	6-2	9-0	11-5	13-11	16-2
	Hem-fir	6-0	8-9	11-1	13-7	15-9
	Southern pine	5-7	8-4	10-7	12-6	14-9
	Spruce-pine-fir	6-1	8-11	11-3	13-9	15-11
24	Douglas fir-larch	5-6	8-1	10-3	12-6	14-6
	Hem-fir	5-4	7-10	9-11	12-1	14-1
	Southern pine	5-0	7-5	9-5	11-3	13-2
	Spruce-pine-fir	5-5	7-11	10-1	12-4	14-3

Table 8.7 Rafter spans for common lumber species, No. 2 grade

(ground snow load = 30 psf, ceiling attached to rafters, L/240, dead load = 10 psf)

Rafter spacing (in.)	Species	Dead load = 10 psf				
		2 × 4	2 × 6	2 × 8	2 × 10	2 × 12
		Maximum rafter spans				
		(ft.-in.)	(ft.-in.)	(ft.-in.)	(ft.-in.)	(ft.-in.)
12	Douglas fir-larch	8-7	13-6	17-8	21-7	25-1
	Hem-fir	8-0	12-7	16-7	21-0	24-4
	Southern pine	8-3	12-11	16-4	19-5	22-10
	Spruce-pine-fir	8-3	12-11	17-0	21-4	24-8
16	Douglas fir-larch	7-10	12-1	15-4	18-9	21-8
	Hem-fir	7-3	11-5	14-11	18-2	21-1
	Southern pine	7-6	11-2	14-2	16-10	19-10
	Spruce-pine-fir	7-6	11-9	15-1	18-5	21-5
19.2	Douglas fir-larch	7-4	11-0	14-0	17-1	19-10
	Hem-fir	6-10	10-9	13-7	16-7	19-3
	Southern pine	6-10	10-2	12-11	15-4	18-1
	Spruce-pine-fir	7-0	10-11	13-9	16-10	19-6
24	Douglas fir-larch	6-9	9-10	12-6	15-3	17-9
	Hem-fir	6-4	9-7	12-2	14-10	17-3
	Southern pine	6-1	9-2	11-7	13-9	16-2
	Spruce-pine-fir	6-6	9-9	12-4	15-1	17-6

Table 8.8 Rafter spans for common lumber species, No. 2 grade
(ground snow load = 50 psf, ceiling attached to rafters, L/240, dead load = 10 psf)

Rafter spacing (in.)	Species	Dead load = 10 psf				
		2 × 4	2 × 6	2 × 8	2 × 10	2 × 12
		Maximum rafter spans				
		(ft.-in.)	(ft.-in.)	(ft.-in.)	(ft.-in.)	(ft.-in.)
12	Douglas fir-larch	7-3	11-5	14-5	17-8	20-5
	Hem-fir	6-9	10-8	14-0	17-2	19-11
	Southern pine	6-11	10-6	13-4	15-10	18-8
	Spruce-pine-fir	6-11	10-11	14-3	17-5	20-2
16	Douglas fir-larch	6-7	9-10	12-6	15-3	17-9
	Hem-fir	6-2	9-7	12-2	14-10	17-3
	Southern pine	6-1	9-2	11-7	13-9	16-2
	Spruce-pine-fir	6-4	9-9	12-4	15-1	17-6
19.2	Douglas fir-larch	6-2	9-0	11-5	13-11	16-2
	Hem-fir	5-9	8-9	11-1	13-7	15-9
	Southern pine	5-7	8-4	10-7	12-6	14-9
	Spruce-pine-fir	5-11	8-11	11-3	13-9	15-11
24	Douglas fir-larch	5-6	8-1	10-3	12-6	14-6
	Hem-fir	5-4	7-10	9-11	12-1	14-1
	Southern pine	5-0	7-5	9-5	11-3	13-2
	Spruce-pine-fir	5-5	7-11	10-1	12-4	14-3

- The ridge board must be at least 1 in. nominal thickness and at least as deep as the cut end of the rafter.
- Valley and hip rafters must be at least 2 in. nominal thickness, adequately supported, and at least as deep as the cut end of the rafter.

Note: For roof slopes of less than 3:12, structural members that support rafters and ceiling joists (such as hips and valleys) must be designed the same as beams.

Headers and Trimmers

Header and trimmer requirements for roof and ceiling openings are as follows:

- Headers longer than 4 ft. must be at least double members.
- Trimmers supporting headers longer than 4 ft. must be at least double members.
- Headers and tail joists require hangers or other methods of support at bearing ends.

Framing Connections

The IRC prescribes minimum framing connections to resist the outward thrust of rafters at the wall top plate and to ensure adequate transfer of all loads to the supporting structure.

- Ceiling joists and rafters must be nailed together.
- Rafters must be fastened to the top wall plate.

- Ceiling joists must provide a continuous tie across the building at the top plate.
- Minimum 2 × 4 rafter ties must be installed if ceiling joists are not connected to the rafters at the plate or if they are installed perpendicular to the rafters.
- Where there are no ceiling joists or rafter ties, the ridge must be supported by a bearing wall or a girder or it must be designed as a beam.
- Rafters and ceiling joists require 1½ in. of bearing on wood or metal and 3 in. on masonry.
- Connections must provide a continuous load path from the roof to the foundation.

Cutting and Notching

Notches in lumber ceiling joists, rafters, and beams are limited as follows (fig. 8.1):

- Depth less than or equal to ⅙ the depth of the member (no more than ¼ at ends)
- Length no longer than ⅓ the depth of the member
- Not located in the middle ⅓ of the span

Holes in ceiling joists, rafters, and beams shall be

- Less than or equal in diameter to ⅓ the depth of the member
- At least 2 in. from the top and bottom of the member
- At least 2 in. away from any other hole or notch

Cuts, notches, and holes in engineered wood products (trusses, structural composite lumber, structural glue-laminated members, or I-joists) are prohibited unless they are

- Permitted by the manufacturer's recommendations
- Part of a specific designed alteration by a registered design professional

Figure 8.1 Cutting, notching, and drilling

Wood Trusses

Wood trusses are to be designed according to accepted engineering practice and referenced standards. Trusses may not be altered without the approval of a registered design professional.

- Truss design drawings are to be
  - Submitted to the building official and approved prior to installation
  - Delivered to the jobsite with the trusses
- Trusses must be braced in accordance with the truss design drawings.

Roof Tie-Down

Roof-to-wall connections to resist wind uplift forces are one component of a complete load path necessary to transmit all loads through the other structural elements to the foundation. The IRC provides prescriptive values for roof uplift resistance based on wind speed, exposure category, and roof span and pitch (table 8.9). The code permits toenails (table 6.1) using three 16d box nails or three 10d common nails to connect the rafter or truss to the top plate under either of the following conditions:

- The tabular value does not exceed 200 pounds, or

■ All of the following apply:
  • basic wind speed ≤ 115 mph
  • wind exposure category B
  • roof pitch ≥ 5 / 12
  • roof span ≤ 32 ft.
  • rafter / truss spacing ≤ 24 in. o.c.

Otherwise, the code requires a proprietary connector with a rated capacity meeting or exceeding the value in table 8.9 for connecting each rafter or truss to the wall.

Note: As an alternative to table 8.9, the builder can use the uplift value specified in the truss design drawings for the roof truss-to-wall connection.

Steel Roof Framing

The code contains prescriptive requirements for cold-formed steel roof framing for buildings not greater than 40 × 60 ft., 3 stories high, and with roof slopes of 3:12 to 12:12. These code provisions are limited to sites with an ultimate design wind speed of less than 139 mph and a ground snow load of 70 psf.

Table 8.9 Rafter or truss uplift connection forces from wind (pounds per connection)

Rafter or truss spacing	Roof span (ft.)	Exposure B			
		Ultimate design wind speed V_{ult} (mph)			
		115		130	
		Roof pitch		Roof pitch	
		< 5:12	≥ 5:12	< 5:12	≥ 5:12
24 in. O.C.	12	118	106	190	176
	18	148	132	244	224
	24	178	158	298	274
	28	198	176	334	306
	32	218	194	370	340
	36	240	212	406	372
	42	270	240	460	422
	48	302	268	516	472

Rafter or truss spacing	Roof Span (ft.)	Exposure C			
		Ultimate design wind speed V_{ult} (mph)			
		115		130	
		Roof Pitch		Roof Pitch	
		< 5:12	≥ 5:12	< 5:12	≥ 5:12
24 in. O.C.	12	220	204	322	302
	18	282	262	416	390
	24	346	320	512	478
	28	390	358	578	538
	32	432	398	642	598
	36	474	438	706	658
	42	538	496	804	750
	48	604	556	900	840

Roof Ventilation

The code requires ventilation for each attic or enclosed roof space as follows:

- Ventilation openings must be covered with corrosion-resistant wire mesh, with $1/16$–$1/4$ in. openings.
- Total net free ventilating area must be at least $1/150$ of the area of the space.
- Free ventilating area of at least $1/300$ of the area of the space is permitted when both of the following conditions are satisfied:
  - 40%–50% of the required ventilating area is in the upper portion of the space and eave or cornice vents provide the balance of ventilating area.
  - In Climate Zones 6, 7, and 8, a Class I or Class II vapor retarder is installed on the warm-in-winter side of the ceiling.
- Insulation shall not block the free flow of air.
- For ventilated spaces, the code requires at least 1 in. of air space between the insulation and the roof sheathing.

Unvented Attic

In unvented attics, the roof above the attic space forms the thermal envelope. The IRC requires installation of *air-impermeable insulation* (typically rigid board insulation) directly under or directly above the structural roof sheathing, with no insulation or vapor barrier installed below the unvented attic area. Air permeable insulation may be applied directly below the air-impermeable insulation, provided this application satisfies minimum rigid board or air- impermeable insulation *R-value* based on climate zone (table 8.10).

Note: In Climate Zones 1, 2 and 3, the code permits air-permeable insulation with vapor diffusion ports to control moisture in unvented attics.

Note: The same principles for unvented attics apply to unvented rafter spaces such as occur in cathedral ceilings.

Table 8.10 Insulation for condensation control above unvented attics

Climate zone	Minimum rigid board or air-impermeable insulation R-value
2B and 3B tile roof only	0 (none required)
1, 2A, 2B, 3A, 3B, 3C	R-5
4C	R-10
4A, 4B	R-15
5	R-20
6	R-25
7	R-30
8	R-35

Attic Access

In wood frame construction, attic areas that exceed 30 sq. ft. and are at least 30 in. high require access as follows:

- The rough opening must be at least 22 × 30 in.
- The opening must be in a hallway or other readily accessible location.
- There must be at least 30 in. headroom above the access.

9

Roof Finishing

Roofing design, materials, construction, and assemblies must provide protection from the weather. Roof coverings must be installed according to the code and the manufacturer's instructions. This chapter addresses roofing underlayment, ice barrier, flashing, and asphalt and wood shingles. It also discusses limitations on reroofing.

Flashing Locations and Materials

Flashing must be corrosion-resistant metal at least 0.019 in. (No. 26 galvanized sheet) or other approved material. It must be installed at the following locations:

- At wall and roof intersections
- Where slope or direction changes
- Around roof openings

Note: The code requires installation of a flashing to divert the water away from where the eave of a sloped roof intersects a vertical sidewall.

Ice Barrier

In areas with a history of water damage to structures from ice dams at roof eaves, asphalt shingles, metal roof shingles, mineral-surfaced roll roofing, slate and slate-type shingles, wood shingles and wood shakes require an ice barrier as follows:

- Self-adhering polymer modified bitumen sheet or two layers of cemented underlayment
- Barrier extending from eave to at least 24 in. inside the exterior wall line of the building.

Note: The ice barrier is not required for unheated detached accessory structures.

Asphalt Shingles

Asphalt shingles must be installed according to the manufacturer's instructions, using special methods of fastening for slopes greater than 21:12. The minimum roof slope is 2:12.

Fasteners

Fasteners must be galvanized steel, stainless steel, aluminum, or copper roofing nails that meet the following minimum size requirements:

- 12 gage (0.105 in.) shank
- 3/8 in. diameter head
- Penetrate at least 3/4 in. into roof sheathing or through sheathing

Underlayment

Approved asphalt-saturated organic felt or other approved material must be installed under shingles. The underlayment lap requirements vary by roof slope and are as follows:

- Slopes of at least 2:12 and less than 4:12 require two layers with 19 in. overlaps.
- Slopes of 4:12 or greater require a single layer with a horizontal lap of at least 2 in.
- End laps are 4 in. and offset at least 6 ft. in adjacent rows

Valleys

Approved valley linings are to be installed according to the manufacturer's installation instructions and must meet one of the following requirements:

- Metal valley lining at least 24 in. wide for open or closed valley
- Two plies of mineral surfaced roll roofing (18 in. bottom, 36 in. top layer) for open or closed valley

Other valley linings for closed valleys (covered with shingles) may include:

- One ply of approved smooth roll roofing at least 36 in. wide
- Self-adhering polymer-modified bitumen sheet

Sidewall Flashing

Where the roof joins a sidewall, the IRC requires step flashings or a continuous flashing measuring at least 4 in. wide by 4 in. high. The flashing at the lower end must turn out to direct water away from the wall.

Drip Edge

The code requires a drip edge at eaves and gables (rakes) of shingle roofs. The drip edge must be installed as follows:

- Minimum lap of 2 in.
- Minimum 0.25 in. extension past roof sheathing
- Minimum 2 in. extension onto roof sheathing
- Maximum 12 in. spacing of fasteners (roofing nails)
- Underlayment over drip edge at eaves
- Underlayment under drip edge at gables (rakes)

Crickets and Saddles

Any chimney penetration more than 30 in. wide requires a cricket or saddle using the same material as the roof covering or sheet metal.

Wood Shingles and Wood Shakes

The IRC includes requirements specific to wood shingles and shakes used for roofing. In addition to material and grading requirements, the code provides installation details related to slope, decking, underlayment, laps, exposure, and fastening.

Application

- Spacing between shingles is ¼–⅜ in.
- Spacing between shakes is ⅜–⅝ in.
- Side laps are offset at least 2½ in. on adjacent courses.
- Each shake or shingle gets two corrosion-resistant fasteners.
- Fasteners are to penetrate sheathing at least ¾ in or through the sheathing.
- Shingle fasteners must be no farther than ¾ in. from the edge and no higher than 1 in. above the exposure line.
- Shake fasteners must be no farther than 1 in. from the edge and no higher than 2 in. above the exposure line.
- Bottom courses are doubled.
- Shakes require 18-in.-wide *interlayment* of No. 30 felt at each course.

Deck requirements

The code permits solid or spaced sheathing for wood shingles and shakes as follows:

- Spaced sheathing must be at least 1 × 4 boards spaced on center, equal to the weather exposure, to coincide with the placement of fasteners.
- Solid sheathing is required under ice barrier materials.
- Deck slope must be at least 3:12.

Underlayment

Use approved asphalt-saturated organic felt or other approved material.

Valleys

Valleys require at least No. 26 gage (0.019 in.) corrosion-resistant sheet metal extended 10 in. from the centerline each way for shingles and 11 in. from the centerline each way for shakes. End laps are at least 4 in.

Reroofing

New roof coverings shall not be installed without first removing existing roof coverings if any of the following conditions are true:

- The existing roof is water-soaked or deteriorated such that it is not adequate as a base for additional roofing.
- The existing roof covering is wood shake, slate, clay, cement, or asbestos-cement tile.
- The existing roof has two or more applications.

Note: Metal panel, metal shingle, and concrete and clay tile roof coverings may be installed over existing wood shakes.

10

Chimneys and Fireplaces

This chapter addresses the design and construction of masonry chimneys and fireplaces, including requirements for combustion air supply, clearance to combustibles, and hearth construction. Design also must comply with other structural provisions of the code, including foundation requirements. In general, the manufacturer's instructions and listing govern the installation of approved factory-built fireplaces and chimneys.

Exterior Air Supply

Both factory-built and masonry fireplaces require an exterior air supply to ensure proper fuel combustion. An alternative is mechanical ventilation as long as it is controlled so that the indoor pressure of the room or space is neutral or positive.

Factory-built fireplaces require exterior air ducts that are a listed component of the fireplace and installed according to the fireplace manufacturer's instructions. Listed ducts for masonry fireplaces must be installed according to the terms of their listing and the manufacturer's instructions.

Exterior Air Intake

The exterior air intake must be covered with a corrosion-resistant screen of ¼ in. mesh and shall not be located in the following areas:

- Garage
- Basement
- Elevation higher than the firebox

Masonry Fireplaces

The prescriptive provisions of the IRC address structural support, approved materials, dimensions, and fire safety for masonry fireplaces.

Footings

Footings must be concrete or solid masonry at least 12 in. thick, extending at least 6 in. beyond the face of the fireplace or foundation wall on all sides.

Hearths and Hearth Extensions

Hearths and hearth extensions are constructed of concrete or masonry and must meet the following requirements:

- Supported by noncombustible materials
- Reinforced to carry their own weight and all loads.
- Hearths constructed at least 4 in. thick
- Hearth extensions constructed at least:
  - 2 in. thick
  - 16 in. in front of fireplace opening
  - 8 in. beyond each side of the fireplace opening

  Note: If the firebox opening is at least 8 in. above the hearth extension, ⅜-in.-thick brick, concrete, stone, or tile may be used. If the fireplace opening is 6 sq. ft. or larger, the hearth must extend at least 20 in. from the front and at least 12 in. beyond each side of the fireplace opening.

Clearances to Wood and Combustibles

Clearances to wood and other combustibles must be at least 2 in. from the front and sides, and at least 4 in. from the back face. Other requirements are as follows:

- The air space between fireplace and combustibles shall not be filled (except for required noncombustible fireblocking).
- Exposed combustible trim, flooring, sheathing, and siding is permitted to abut the masonry fireplace side walls and hearth extension if these items are at least 12 in. from the inside surface of the nearest firebox lining.

- Exposed combustible mantels or trim installed directly on the masonry fireplace front must be at least 6 in. from the fireplace opening.
- If it is within 12 in. of the fireplace opening, the trim cannot project more than ⅛ in. for each inch of distance from the opening.

Masonry Chimneys

The code prescribes construction details of masonry chimneys for proper drafting, weather protection, and safety from fire.

Seismic Requirements

Four continuous vertical No. 4 reinforcing bars are required for masonry and concrete chimneys up to 40 in. wide with a single flue located in SDC D_0, D_1, or D_2. Additional requirements are as follows:

- Two additional vertical bars for each additional flue or each additional 40 in. of width
- Vertical reinforcing enclosed in ¼ in. horizontal ties every 18 in. vertically
- Two horizontal ties at each bend in vertical bars
- Anchorage to the structure at every floor, ceiling, or roof more than 6 ft. above grade

Termination

Masonry chimneys must terminate at least 3 ft. above the roof and at least 2 ft. higher than any portion of a building within 10 ft. (fig. 10.1). The code requires a chimney cap that meets the following requirements:

- Constructed or manufactured of concrete, metal or stone materials
- Sloped to shed water
- Includes a drip edge
- Has a caulked bond break around any flue liners

Chimneys shall extend at least 2' higher than any portion of a building within 10' and at least 3' above the high point of the roof at the chimney location

Figure 10.1 Figure height above roof

Chimney Clearances

The minimum clearances between masonry chimneys and combustible materials are as follows:

- Air space clearance to combustibles must be at least 2 in. or at least 1 in. if the chimney is located entirely outside the exterior walls of the building.
- The air space between the chimney and combustibles shall not be filled (except for required noncombustible fireblocking).
- Exposed combustible trim, and the edges of flooring, sheathing, and siding are permitted to abut the masonry chimney if these items are at least 8 in. from the inside surface of the nearest flue lining.

Chimney Fireblocking

Noncombustible fireblocking securely anchored in place is required in the concealed spaces at floors and ceilings.

Chimney Crickets

Crickets are required for chimneys 30 in. wide or larger (table 10.1, fig. 10.2).

Table 10.1 Cricket dimensions

Roof slope	Height
12:12	½ of width
8:12	⅓ of width
6:12	¼ of width
4:12	⅙ of width
3:12	⅛ of width

Factory-Built Fireplaces

Factory-built fireplaces and chimneys must be listed and labeled, tested in accordance with UL 127, and installed according to the conditions of the listing.

- Hearth extensions are to be installed in accordance with the listing of the fireplace.
- Hearth extensions must be readily distinguishable from the surrounding floor area.
- Chimney offsets cannot exceed 30 degrees from vertical.
- No more than 4 elbows may be used for chimney offsets.

Figure 10.2 Chimney cricket

Source: International Residential Code for One- and Two-Family Dwellings, 2006. Washington, DC: International Code Council Inc., 2006, p. 310.

11

Energy Efficiency

This chapter addresses the code-prescribed methods to ensure that a home's systems and the entire building thermal envelope—including insulation, doors, windows, and cladding—conserve energy. The energy provisions of the IRC are from the *International Energy Conservation Code* (IECC).[7]

General Requirements

The IRC provides a map and lists the climate zone of each county for determining compliance with the thermal envelope requirements for dwellings. The general provisions for energy efficiency include identification and certification requirements.

Identification

Insulation materials and *fenestration* components must be labeled or identified to verify code compliance as follows:

- The factory-applied R-value mark on insulation is visible after installation.
- There are fixed markers for every 300 sq. ft. of attic space to indicate initial thickness of blown or sprayed roof/ceiling insulation.
- Windows, skylights, and glazed doors are labeled and certified by manufacturer with *U-factor* and *solar heat gain coefficient* (SHGC)

Installer Certification

For insulation products that do not bear a label or mark, the installer must provide certification listing the type, manufacturer, and R-value of insulation. The insulation installer must sign, date, and post the certificate. Certification for blown-in fiberglass or cellulose also must indicate

- Initial installed thickness
- Settled thickness
- Settled R-value
- Installed density
- Coverage area
- Number of bags installed

Permanent Certificate

The code requires the builder or registered design professional to complete a permanent energy efficiency certificate and post the certificate on a wall near the furnace or another approved location inside the building. Where posted on the electrical panel, the certificate cannot cover the service directory or other labels. The certificate must list the following:

- Predominant R-values of insulation installed at the following locations:
  - Ceiling/roof
  - Walls
  - Foundation (walls and slabs)
  - Ducts in unconditioned spaces
- Results of air-leakage testing
  - Blower door test for building envelope
  - Duct system
- U-factors and SHGC of fenestration for the following components:
  - Skylights
  - Windows
  - Doors
  - Glass block
- Type and efficiency of the following equipment:
  - Heating
  - Cooling
  - Water heating
- Information for any on-site photovoltaic panel systems
- Energy Rating Index score when applicable
- The code edition

■ The compliance path used
  • Prescriptive
  • Total Building Performance
  • Energy Rating Index

The following appliances must be listed individually on the certificate without an efficiency designation:
■ Electric furnaces
■ Baseboard heaters
■ Unvented gas-fired heaters

Compliance Paths

The builder may choose one of three paths for demonstrating compliance with the energy provisions as follows:
■ Prescriptive option
■ Total Building Performance option
■ An energy rating index (ERI) option

Additional Requirements

For the prescriptive option, the code requires one of the following additional energy-saving features:
■ Enhanced thermal envelope performance
■ More efficient HVAC equipment (≥ 95 AFUE natural gas furnace and ≥ 16 SEER air conditioner)

- More efficient duct thermal distribution system
- Improved air sealing and efficient ventilation system

Building Thermal Envelope

For following the prescriptive path to compliance, the code provides the minimum thermal envelope ratings by component, based on climate zone (tables 11.1 and 11.2). In addition, the code sets mandatory requirements for reducing and measuring air leakage in the building thermal envelope.

Specific Insulation Requirements

In addition to the component requirements listed in table 11.1, the code offers alternatives to reduce the minimum R-values under specific conditions as follows:

- A reduction in the required ceiling R-value is permitted for raised heel (energy) trusses that allow the full height of uncompressed insulation to extend over the wall top plate at the eaves.
  - R-49 is reduced to R-38.
  - R-60 is reduced to R-49.

Table 11.1 Insulation minimum R-value and fenestration requirements by component

Climate zone	Ceiling R-Value	Wood frame wall R-value		Floor R-Value	Basement and crawl space wall R-Value		Slab	
		Cavity	Plus Continuous		Cavity	Or Continuous	R-value	Depth (ft.)
1	30	13	0	13	0	0	0	0
2	49	13	0	13	0	0	0	0
3	49	20	0	19	13	5	0	0
4 except Marine	60	20	0	19	13	10	10	2
5 and Marine 4	60	20	0	30	19	15	10	2
6	60	20	5	30	19	15	10	4
7 and 8	60	20	5	30	19	15	10	4

Table 11.2 Fenestration requirements by component

Climate Zone	Fenestration U-Factor	Skylight U-Factor	Glazed fenestration SHGC
1	NR	0.75	0.25
2	0.40	0.65	0.25
3	0.30	0.55	0.25
4 except Marine	0.30	0.55	0.40
5 and Marine 4	0.30	0.55	0.40
6	0.30	0.55	NR*
7 and 8	0.30	0.55	NR*

*NR: No requirement

- Ceiling insulation values greater than R-30 may be reduced to R-30 for not more than 500 sq. ft. of ceiling area if there is insufficient space for the required insulation.
- Floor insulation values greater than R-19 may be reduced to R-19 if the cavity is filled with insulation.
- The code provides insulation values for mass walls (typically above-grade concrete or concrete-block walls) and increases the required R-value when more than 50% of the insulation is on the inside of the wall.

222 HOME BUILDERS' JOBSITE CODES

Other specific insulation requirements are as follows:

- Slab-on-grade floors less than 12 in. below grade must be insulated inside or outside of the foundation wall.
  - Vertical and horizontal insulation may be combined to achieve the required depth of insulation.
  - Slab-edge insulation is not required in jurisdictions designated as very heavy termite infestation areas.
- Unvented crawl space wall insulation (when floor above is not insulated) must cover the wall and extend an additional 24 in. vertically or horizontally at the base.
- Exposed earth of crawl space must have a vapor retarder attached to stem walls with 6 in. sealed overlaps.
- Horizontal access hatches from conditioned to unconditioned spaces such as attics and crawl spaces require insulation, weather stripping, and a means to preserve the surrounding insulation R-value when accessing equipment.
- The maximum fenestration U-factors apply to vertical access doors from conditioned to unconditioned spaces.

Note: The code permits reduced R-values for horizontal pull-down, stair-type access hatches in climate zones 0 through 4.

Air Leakage

The building thermal envelope must be sealed at the following locations:

- Air barrier joints, seams, and penetrations (including utility penetrations)
- Windows, skylights and doors
- Junctions and breaks in walls, floors and ceilings
- Garage separation
- Behind tubs and showers on exterior walls
- Access openings and doors to unconditioned spaces
- Foundation and sill plate junction
- Rim joists junctions
- Recessed lighting
- Electrical and communication boxes
- Plumbing and wiring
- HVAC register boots
- Concealed sprinklers
- Other sources of infiltration

Note: Electrical and communication outlet boxes in the thermal envelope must be tested and marked in compliance with NEMA OS 4, "Requirements for Air-Sealed Boxes for Electrical and Communication Applications."

Fireplaces

New wood-burning fireplaces require tight-fitting flue dampers or doors and outdoor combustion air. Tight-fitting doors require listing and labeling to the applicable standard.

Recessed lighting

When located in the building thermal envelope, recessed *luminaires* must meet the following criteria:

- IC (insulation contact) rated
- Labeled as meeting ASTM E 283 to reduce air leakage as follows:
  - tested at 1.57 psi pressure differential
  - no more than 2.0 *cfm* air movement
- Gasket or caulk applied between housing and interior wall or ceiling covering

Testing of the Thermal Envelope

The code requires a blower door test on every dwelling unit to verify compliance with air leakage limitations. The test pressure is 0.2 in. water gage (50 pascals). For the prescriptive path, the maximum air leakage rate is

- 5 ACH in Climate Zones 1 and 2
- 3 ACH in Climate Zones 3 through 8

Systems

The IRC regulates certain components of mechanical systems and controls to conserve energy.

Thermostats

The code requires a programmable thermostat for the primary heating or cooling system.

Ducts

To conserve energy, ducts must be insulated and sealed as follows:

- Ducts 3 in. in diameter and larger in unconditioned spaces require at least R-8 insulation.
- Ducts less than 3 in. in diameter in unconditioned spaces require at least R-6 insulation.
- The following require sealing:
  - Ducts
  - Air handlers
  - Filter boxes

Note: Building framing cavities are not permitted to be supply or return air ducts.

Duct Testing

Unless ducts and air handlers are located entirely within the building thermal envelope, the code requires pressure testing at either the rough-in stage or after construction.

Hot Water Pipe Insulation

The code requires R-3 insulation on hot water piping that

- Is located outside the conditioned space
- Travels from the water heater to a distribution manifold
- Is under a floor slab or otherwise buried
- Is part of a recirculation system other than a demand recirculation system

Mechanical Ventilation

The IRC energy provisions require mechanical ventilation as follows:

- A whole-house mechanical ventilation system or other approved ventilation
- Outdoor air intakes and exhausts to have automatic or gravity dampers
- Energy efficient ventilation fans that meet the minimum efficacy (cfm/watt) requirements
- A heat recovery or energy recovery ventilation system in Climate Zones 7 and 8
- Testing of system

Swimming Pools

The IRC requires that heated swimming pools include these energy-conserving measures:

- A readily accessible on-off switch for pool heaters
- No continuously burning pilot lights on gas-fired heaters
- Automatic time switches for pool heaters
- A vapor retardant pool cover on the water surface

Lighting Systems

The energy provisions require the following features related to lighting systems:

- High-efficacy lamps in all permanent lighting fixtures
- Dimmer, occupant sensor or other control for most interior permanent lighting fixtures
  - Not applicable to bathrooms, hallways, exterior or security lighting
- Exterior lighting (total 30 watts or more)
  - Controlled by manual switch that permits automatic shut-off
  - Automatic shut off during daylight

12

Mechanical Systems

This chapter addresses the mechanical (heating, ventilation, and air-conditioning, or HVAC) section of the code, which regulates the safe installation of equipment and systems that control environmental conditions of a dwelling, such as comfort heating, cooling, and ventilation, including solid- or liquid-fuel appliances. *(See chapter 13 for information on installing gas-fired appliances.)* Equipment and systems outside the scope of the IRC must comply with the applicable provisions of the *International Mechanical Code*[8] and the *International Fuel Gas Code.*[9]

General Requirements

HVAC appliances must

- Be listed and labeled for the intended application
- Carry the permanent factory-applied nameplate, including the mark of the approved testing agency

- Include the manufacturer's operating and installation instructions attached to the appliance.

Drilling and Notching

To preserve the structural integrity of the framing system, drilling and notching of wood framing is limited to locations and dimensions as specified in chapters 5, 6, and 8 of this publication (on floors, walls, and roofs). Concealed piping that is less than 1½ in. from the nearest edge of a framing member must be protected from fastener penetration by shield plates that are at least 0.0575-in.-thick steel (No. 16 gage).

Note: Cast iron and galvanized steel pipe resist fastener penetration so they do not require additional protection.

Access to Appliances

Appliances require access for service, repair, and replacement, and must maintain minimum clearances as follows:

- 30 × 30 in. working space in front of control side of the appliance
- Clearance to combustibles in accordance with the appliance's label and the manufacturer's instructions

- The access door and passageway to the appliance must be
  - At least 24 in. wide
  - Large enough to remove the largest appliance

Appliances in Attics

For maintenance or replacement of appliances installed in attics, the code requires an access opening and passageway large enough to remove the largest piece of equipment. Additional requirements are as follows:

- The attic access opening must be at least 30 × 20 in.
- The continuous solid floor of the passageway must be at least 24 in. wide.
- The passageway must be at least 22 in. wide × 30 in. high and not more than 20 ft. long.
- A receptacle outlet and switch-controlled light must be located near the appliance.
- There must be a light switch at the access opening.

Note: An unobstructed passageway that is at least 6 ft. high may extend 50 ft.

Appliance Installation

Installations must conform to the listing, label, and manufacturer's instructions. Installation also must include protection from ignition hazards, physical damage, and corrosion.

Appliances in Garages

For appliances installed in a garage, the IRC requires any ignition source, such as a pilot or electrical switching device, to be at least 18 in. above the floor. *Note: Appliances that are listed as flammable-vapor-ignition resistant do not require elevation of the ignition source.*

Protection from Impact

The code provides for protection of appliances against accidental physical damage from impact by vehicles. Appliances in any location subject to moving vehicles, such as in garages or outdoors adjacent to driveways, require one of the following means of protection:

- Steel pipe bollards
- Curbs
- Other approved barriers

Note: Suspended appliances with sufficient clearance above the floor and appliances installed in an alcove out of the path of vehicle travel are not subject to impact and do not require additional barriers.

Clearance above Grade

Appliances supported from the ground require a level concrete slab or other approved base that is at least 3 in. above grade.

Condensate

Condensate from cooling coils or evaporators must drain to an approved location.

- An auxiliary drain system is required in areas where cooling condensate overflow would damage building components (such as in an attic installation above finished space). Use one of the following methods:
  - An auxiliary drain pan with a separate drain
  - A separate overflow drain line connected to the equipment drain pan that discharges to a conspicuous location
  - Water level detection to shut off equipment, located either in the primary drain line or in an auxiliary drain pan.
- Approved condensate drain piping is at least ¾ in. internal diameter.

Note: Condensate pumps in uninhabitable spaces require interconnection with the equipment to prevent appliance operation if the pump fails.

Exhaust Systems

Mechanical exhaust systems must discharge to the outside air and are not allowed to exhaust into an attic, soffit, ridge vent, or crawl space. In addition, exhaust terminations must maintain a clearance of at least 3 ft. to openings into the building, such as windows, doors, and fresh air intakes.

Clothes Dryer Exhaust Systems

Dryer exhaust systems must
- Be independent of all other systems
- Convey moisture to the outdoors
- Terminate outside at least 3 ft. from openings into buildings or per manufacturer's instructions
- Have a backdraft damper and no screen at the exhaust termination

The dryer exhaust duct system must meet the following requirements:
- 4 in. nominal in diameter
- At least 0.016-in.-thick smooth, rigid metal
- Joints pointed in the direction of air flow
- Mechanical fastening with penetration into the duct of not more than ⅛ in.
- Sealed joints

■ Duct supports spaced not more than 12 ft.

Note: The code permits a single listed and labeled transition duct not more than 8 ft. long between the dryer and the exhaust duct. The transition duct cannot be concealed.

Dryer Exhaust Duct Installation

The code requires the following for dryer duct installation:

■ No longer than 35 ft. (unless the manufacturer permits a longer length)

■ Length reductions for fittings per table 12.1

■ Permanent label or tag identifying the length of duct exceeding 35 ft.

■ Protection of a concealed duct that is less than 1¼ in. from the edge of framing

Note: The code permits the installation of a listed dryer exhaust duct power ventilator to increase the length of the dryer duct in accordance with the manufacturer's instructions. Domestic booster fans are not permitted for this purpose.

Kitchen Range Hoods

Domestic open-top broiler units require an overhead metal exhaust hood unless the unit is equipped with a listed integral system. This hood is not required for other domestic kitchen cooking appliances. However,

Table 12.1 Dryer exhaust duct fitting equivalent length

Dryer exhaust duct fitting type	Equivalent length	
	(ft.)	(in.)
4" radius mitered 45° elbow	2	6
4" radius mitered 90° elbow	5	0
6" radius smooth 45° elbow	1	0
6" radius smooth 90° elbow	1	9
8" radius smooth 45° elbow	1	0
8" radius smooth 90° elbow	1	7
10" radius smooth 45° elbow	0	9
10" radius smooth 90° elbow	1	6

when it is installed, it must comply with manufacturer's instructions. Kitchen exhaust rates must comply with table 12.2. Other specific requirements follow:

- A single-wall, smooth, airtight duct of galvanized steel, stainless steel, or copper (*PVC* pipe permitted for downdraft systems) is required.
- The exhaust system cannot terminate in crawl space or attic.
- The duct must terminate outdoors with a backdraft damper.

Note: Listed ductless range hoods are not required to discharge to outdoors.

Makeup Air

For kitchen range hood systems capable of exhausting more than 400 cfm, the code requires mechanical or natural makeup air at a rate approximately equal to the exhaust rate.

Note: Makeup air is not required if all fuel-burning appliances are direct-vent or mechanical draft vent.

Mechanical Ventilation

When installed, local exhaust and whole-house mechanical ventilation must comply with the minimum ventilation airflow rates of the code.

Bathrooms and Toilet Rooms with Mechanical Ventilation

Local exhaust systems must meet the following requirements:

■ Exhaust must terminate outdoors.
■ Exhaust cannot recirculate.
■ Ventilation rates must comply with table 12.2.

Table 12.2 Minimum required local exhaust rates

Area to be exhausted	Exhaust rates
Kitchens	100 cfm intermittent or 25 cfm continuous
Bathrooms and toilet rooms	Mechanical exhaust capacity of 50 cfm intermittent or 20 cfm continuous

Whole-House Mechanical Ventilation System

The energy provisions require a whole-house mechanical ventilation system (or approved equivalent) for every dwelling unit. The code permits local exhaust or supply fans, or a combination, to serve as such a system. An out-door air duct connected to the return side of an air handler is one approved method for providing supply ventilation. The whole-house ventilation system must supply air at the minimum continuous rate specified (table 12.3) or the minimum intermittent rate (table 12.4).

Note: The code allows a 30 percent reduction to the mechanical ventilation airflow rate for balanced ventilation systems.

Table 12.3 Continuous whole-house mechanical ventilation system airflow rate requirements

Dwelling unit floor area (sq. ft.)	Number of bedrooms				
	0–1	2–3	4–5	6–7	> 7
	Airflow in CFM				
< 1,500	30	45	60	75	90
1,501–3,000	45	60	75	90	105
3,001–4,500	60	75	90	105	120
4,501–6,000	75	90	105	120	135
6,001–7,500	90	105	120	135	150
> 7,500	105	120	135	150	165

Table 12.4 Intermittent whole-house mechanical ventilation rate factors

Run-time percentage in each 4-hour segment	25%	33%	50%	66%	75%	100%
Factor	4	3	2	1.5	1.3	1.0

Note: The code permits intermittent operation when the system can be set to operate at least 25% of each 4-hour segment and the ventilation rate prescribed in table 12.3 is multiplied by the factor in table 12.4.

Duct Systems

The IRC sets requirements for the materials, fabrication, and installation of duct systems as follows:

- Approved materials meeting the temperature and flame-spread ratings of the code
- Factory-made ducts listed and labeled to applicable UL standards
- Airtight joints and seams
- Maximum flame-spread of 25 and smoke-developed index of 50 for duct insulation
- Labels for external duct insulation with R-value, flame-spread rating, and smoke-developed index
- Maximum 10 ft. spacing of metal duct supports
  - ½ in. wide, 18-gage metal straps

  or
  - 12-gage galvanized wire

Note: The code also permits the use of spray polyurethane foam for insulating and sealing ducts when the foam meets the applicable conditions and specifications.

Return Air Openings

The code restricts the sources of return air to prevent the circulation of unpleasant or noxious odors and to prevent negative pressures in confined spaces or appliance locations. Return air shall not be obtained from the following locations:

- Less than 10 ft. from an open combustion chamber or draft hood of another appliance in the same space
- Another dwelling unit
- Closet, bathroom, *toilet room,* kitchen, garage, mechanical room, boiler room, furnace room or unconditioned attic
- Unconditioned crawl space through a direct connection

Note: The code does not prohibit transfer openings in the crawl space enclosure.

The amount of return air taken from any room shall not exceed the flow rate of supply air to that room.

Combustion Air

Fuel-burning appliances require a supply of air for fuel combustion, draft hood dilution, and ventilation of the space in which the appliance is installed. Combustion air requirements for solid-fuel-burning appliances must follow the manufacturer's installation instructions. Oil-fired appliances require combustion air in accordance with National Fire Protection Association (NFPA) 31.[10] The requirements for combustion and dilution air for gas-fired appliances are in chapter 13 of this publication.

Chimneys and Vents for Solid-Fuel and Oil-Burning Appliances

The code prohibits connecting a solid-fuel-burning appliance or fireplace to a chimney that vents another appliance.

Ranges and Ovens

The IRC regulates the installation of household cooking appliances as follows:

- Freestanding or built-in ranges require at least 30 in. of clearance from unprotected combustible material located above the cooking top.
- A reduced clearance is permitted if it complies with the listing and labeling of the range hood or appliance.
- Cooking appliances must be listed and labeled for household use, and installed according to the manufacturer's instructions.

13

Fuel Gas

This chapter addresses the safe installation of gas-fired appliances and fuel-gas piping systems, including requirements for combustion and ventilation air, venting, and connections. (Liquid- and solid-fuel appliances are covered in chapter 12.) The IRC includes excerpts from the *International Fuel Gas Code*,[11] which may be used for installations outside the scope of the IRC.

General

Appliance installation requirements include provisions for preventing damage to building components.

- Appliances must be listed and labeled for the specific intended purpose.
- An auxiliary drain pan is required for Category IV condensing appliances where overflow would damage any part of the building, such as where a furnace is installed in an attic above living space.

Note: *The auxiliary pan is not required if the appliance has a device to shut the appliance down automatically if the primary drain becomes clogged.*

Note: *Condensate pumps in uninhabitable spaces such as attics or crawl spaces require interconnection with the equipment to prevent appliance operation if the pump fails.*

Appliance Location

In addition to the code requirements, appliance location depends on the conditions of its listing. Gas-fired appliances installed in sleeping rooms, bathrooms, toilet rooms, or storage closets, or in a space that opens only into these rooms or spaces, are limited to the following specific installations. Otherwise, gas-fired appliances are prohibited in these rooms or areas.

- Direct-vent appliances are permitted if they are installed according to the manufacturer's instructions.
- A gas dryer is permitted in a bathroom or toilet room if an air transfer opening to another space is provided. The opening cannot communicate with a bathroom, toilet room, bedroom or closet.
- Vented room heaters, wall furnaces, vented decorative appliances, and vented gas fireplaces are permitted in rooms that meet the required volume for indoor combustion air.

- A single unvented room heater may be permitted in a bathroom or bedroom, subject to input rating limitations, combustion air volumes, and required automatic oxygen depletion safety shutoff systems
- An appliance is permitted in a room or space that opens only into a bedroom or bathroom under the following conditions:
  - The space is used for no other purpose.
  - A solid, weather-stripped, self-closing door is installed.
  - All combustion air is taken directly from the outdoors.

Combustion, Ventilation, and Dilution Air

Gas-fired appliances require an air supply for fuel combustion, draft hood dilution, and ventilation of the space in which the appliance is installed. Combustion air requirements for solid- and liquid- fuel burning appliances appear in the mechanical section of the code and are covered in chapter 12 of this publication.

- In addition to the code requirements, combustion, ventilation, and dilution air must meet the appliance manufacturer's instructions.
- Exhaust fans, ventilation systems, clothes dryers, and fireplaces require makeup air only if they interfere with the operation of appliances.

Indoor Combustion Air

The code permits combustion air to be obtained from inside the building under the following conditions:

- The minimum required volume of air is 50 cu. ft. per 1,000 *Btu/h*.
- Openings used to connect indoor spaces to obtain the required volume of indoor combustion air must be sized and located as follows (fig. 13.1):
  - Each opening requires a free area of 1 sq. in. per 1,000 Btu/h and at least 100 sq. in.
  - One opening must begin within 12 in. of the top and one opening must begin within 12 in. of the bottom of the enclosure.

Outdoor Combustion Air Obtained through Two Openings or Ducts

This option for necessary combustion air connects the space containing the appliance to the outdoors through two openings or ducts.

- One opening is to begin within 12 in. of the top of the enclosure and one within 12 in. of the bottom (fig. 13.2).
- Openings are permitted to connect to spaces directly communicating with the outdoors, such as ventilated crawl spaces or ventilated attic spaces.

One of the required openings is within 12 in. of the ceiling

Two permanent openings 1 sq. in. per 1,000 Btu/h for each opening (min. area for each opening is 100 sq. in.)

One of the required openings is within 12 in. of the floor

furnace

confined space

Figure 13.1 All combustion air from indoors

Source: 2006 International Residential Code Study Companion. Washington, DC: International Code Council, 2006, p.290.

Figure 13.2 All combustion air from outdoors

Source: 2006 International Residential Code Study Companion. Washington, DC: International Code Council, 2006, p. 292.

- Sizes of openings are as follows:
  - For direct openings to outdoors or vertical ducts, the free area of each duct must be at least 1 sq. in. per 4,000 Btu/h of total input rating.
  - For horizontal ducts, the free area of each opening must be at least 1 sq. in. per 2,000 Btu/h of total input rating.

Outdoor Combustion Air Obtained through Single Opening or Duct

As an alternative to two openings, the code permits a single opening to supply combustion air from the outdoors, provided the opening is increased in size and meets other requirements as follows:

- The opening must begin within 12 in. of the top of the enclosure (fig. 13.3).
- Free area is to be at least 1 sq. in. per 3,000 Btu/h of the total input rating.
- Free area must equal at least the sum of the areas of all vent connectors in the space.

Combination Indoor and Outdoor Combustion Air

The calculated size of outdoor openings may be reduced by a factor based on a ratio of available interior air volume divided by the required volume of combustion air.

Figure 13.3 All combustion air from outdoors through one opening

Source: 2006 International Residential Code Study Companion. Washington, DC: International Code Council, 2006, p. 292.

Mechanical Combustion Air Supply

As an alternative to natural infiltration of combustion air, the code permits a mechanical system to bring in combustion air when the following conditions are met:

- Combustion air must be supplied from the outdoors at a rate of at least 0.35 cfm per 1,000 Btu/h.
- Exhaust fans require makeup air.
- Appliances must interlock with the mechanical air supply system.

Louvers and Grilles Net Free Area

When using louvers or grilles to satisfy combustion air requirements, the amount of net free area is as specified by the manufacturer. If the manufacturer's specifications are not known, the amount can be calculated as follows:

- 75% of the gross area for metal louvers
- 25% of the gross area for wood louvers

Combustion Air Ducts

Combustion air ducts must

- Be manufactured of galvanized steel
- Serve only lower or only upper openings (not both)
- Have at least 12 in. clearance above grade for exterior air intake openings

Appliances in Garages

The following requirements apply to appliances
installed in garages:

- The appliance must be protected from automobile
  impact by a barrier, elevation, placement in an
  offset alcove, or by other approved means.
- The ignition source for the appliance must be at
  least 18 in. above the floor.

*Note: The code does not require elevation for appliances
that are listed as flammable-vapor-ignition resistant.*

Exterior Equipment and Appliance Installation

Equipment and appliances installed outdoors must be

- Supported on a level concrete slab or other
  approved material extending at least 3 in. above
  grade, or
- Suspended at least 6 in. above the finished grade

Fuel-Gas Piping

The IRC provides for the design, materials, and
safe installation of fuel-gas piping to serve gas-fired
appliances.

Pipe Sizing

Gas piping is sized to supply adequate volume to meet the demand of the connected appliances. Appliance input ratings, type of gas (natural or liquid petroleum), type of pipe, length of pipe, inlet pressure, and pressure drop are among the factors that determine proper pipe size. The code includes pipe sizing tables and sizing equations, but permits other approved methods for sizing gas pipe.

Piping Materials

The IRC permits any of the following materials for gas piping:

- Steel pipe not lighter than Schedule 10
- Approved seamless metallic tubing if gas used is not corrosive to the material
- Corrugated stainless steel tubing (CSST) Approved polyethylene plastic pipe, tubing, and fittings for outdoor underground installations

Piping System Prohibited Locations

The code does not permit gas piping in the following locations:

- Supply, return, or exhaust duct
- Clothes chute
- Chimney or gas vent
- Through any townhome unit other than the unit being served

Shield Plate Requirements

Concealed piping installed less than 1½ in. from the nearest edge of the framing member must be protected from fastener penetration by shield plates that are at least 00.0575-in.-thick (No. 16 gage) steel. *Note: Black and galvanized steel pipe do not require protection.*

Other Installation Requirements

Gas piping must be inspected and pressure tested before it is concealed or put into service. The following requirements apply to gas piping in outdoor or underground locations:

- Aboveground piping outdoors must be at least 3½ in. above ground and above roof surfaces.
- Exposed exterior ferrous metal piping must be protected from corrosion.
- Underground piping must be corrosion resistant and approved for the location or have a factory-applied, electrically-insulating coating.
  Note: Galvanizing is not considered adequate protection for underground installation.
- Underground piping must be buried at least 12 in.
- Gas piping must not penetrate foundation walls underground.

Appliance Connections

Connectors are not allowed to pass through walls, floors, partitions, ceilings, or appliance housings (other than connectors to fireplace inserts with proper grommets in accordance with the manufacturer's instructions). Connector length is limited to no more than 6 ft. The following are approved for appliance connection to the gas piping system:

- Rigid metallic pipe and fittings
- CSST
- Listed and labeled appliance connectors

Shutoff Valve

Each appliance requires a shutoff valve and, except for alternate provisions that apply to decorative appliances and fireplaces, the valve is to be

- Upstream of the connector
- Accessible and in the same room as the appliance
- Within 6 ft. of the appliance

Note: In a manifold system, the shutoff valve may be located at the manifold and up to 50 ft. from the appliance when the shutoff valve is readily accessible and permanently identified.

Note: Shutoff valves for movable appliances, such as cooking appliances and clothes dryers, are permitted to be installed behind the appliances and still meet the access requirements.

Sediment Trap

A sediment trap is required downstream of the shutoff valve and adjacent to the inlet of equipment, except for

- Illuminating appliances
- Ranges
- Clothes dryers
- Outdoor grills
- Gas fireplaces

Piping Support

See table 13.1 for maximum spacing of supports for gas piping. CSST supports must follow the manufacturer's instructions.

Table 13.1 Support of fuel-gas piping

Steel pipe, nominal size of pipe (in.)	Spacing of supports (ft.)	Nominal size of tubing smooth-wall (in., outside diameter)	Spacing of supports (ft.)
½	6	½	4
¾ or 1	8	⅝ or ¾	6
1¼ or larger (horizontal)	10	⅞ or 1 (horizontal)	8
1¼ or larger (vertical)	Every floor level	1 or larger (vertical)	Every floor level

Vents

Gas appliances must vent to the atmosphere to release their combustion products. Vents must
- Be listed and labeled for use with the type of appliance (except plastic piping used to vent *Category IV appliances*)
- Have appropriate clearance to combustibles as specified by the manufacturer
- Have a 0.0187 in. (26 gage) sheet metal insulation shield that terminates at least 2 in. above insulation in attic if vents pass through insulated assemblies

Where vents are installed in concealed locations through holes or notches in framing, and are less than 1½ in. from the edge of the framing, the vents require protection from fastener penetration by installing a fastener shield plate of 00.057-in.-thick (16 gage) steel. The shield plate must
- Cover the vent area at the framing
- Ensure at least 4 in. of protection above the bottom plates, below the top plates, and to each side of a stud, joist, or rafter

Gas Vent Roof Termination

The required termination height for gas vents of no more than 12 in. and at least 8 ft. from a vertical wall is based on the roof pitch (table 13.2 and fig. 13.4). Gas vents larger than 12 in. or less than 8 ft. from a vertical wall must terminate at least 2 ft. above the roof and any portion of a building that is

Table 13.2 Gas vent termination locations (Minimum height from roof to lowest discharge opening) for listed caps 12 in. or smaller, at least 8 ft. from a vertical wall

Roof slope	Minimum height in ft.
Flat to 6/12	1.0
> 6/12 to 7/12	1.25
> 7/12 to 8/12	1.5
> 8/12 to 9/12	2.0
> 9/12 to 10/12	2.5
> 10/12 to 11/12	3.25
> 11/12 to 12/12	4.0
> 12/12 to 14/12	5.0
> 14/12 to 16/12	6.0
> 16/12 to 18/12	7.0
> 18/12 to 20/12	7.5
> 20/12 to 21/12	8.0

within 10 ft. horizontally. In addition, gas vent roof termination must include

- Roof flashing or roof jack
- Listed termination cap

Note: Vent terminals require a minimum 12 in. horizontal clearance from the swing of a door.

Figure 13.4 Gas vent termination locations (for listed caps 12 in. or smaller, at least 8 ft. from a vertical wall)

Source: International Residential Code for One- and Two-Family Dwellings, 2006. Washington, DC: International Code Council Inc., 2006, p. 400.

Mechanical Draft Venting System Termination

Mechanical draft venting systems must terminate at least 3 ft. above any forced-air inlet located within 10 ft. For other than direct vent appliances, mechanical draft venting systems must meet the following termination clearances:

- At least 4 ft. below, 4 ft. horizontally from, and 1 ft. above any door, operable window, or gravity air inlet in the building
- At least 12 in. above grade

Direct-Vent Appliance Vent Termination

Through-the-wall, direct-vent appliance vents must terminate at least

- 6 in. from any air opening into the building when appliance input is less than or equal to 10,000 Btu/h
- 9 in. from any air opening into the building when appliance input is greater than 10,000 but not more than 50,000 Btu/h
- 12 in. from any air opening into the building when appliance input is more than 50,000 Btu/h

Gas Clothes Dryer Exhaust

The system must follow manufacturer's instructions, be independent of all other systems, and

- Convey moisture and combustion products to the outside
- Have an outside termination equipped with a backdraft damper and no screens
- Include the required makeup air for exhaust greater than 200 cfm or for closet enclosures
- Have a nominal 4 in. diameter smooth, rigid metal dryer duct of at least 0.016-in.-thick material supported at 4 ft. intervals
- Have duct ends inserted into adjoining duct or fitting in the direction of air flow
- Not have screws or fasteners penetrating into duct more than ⅛ in.

Note: The code permits a single listed and labeled transition duct no longer than 8 ft. to connect the dryer to the exhaust duct system. The transition duct cannot be concealed within construction.

Protection of Dryer Exhaust Duct

The code requires shield plates to protect dryer exhaust duct from nail or screw penetration where there is less than 1¼ in. between the duct and the face of the framing member. Shield plates must comply with the following:

- Be constructed of steel at least 0.062 in. thick
- Extend at least 2 in. above sole plates and below top plates

Dryer Exhaust Duct Length

Unless the manufacturer's instructions permit a longer length, the IRC limits a gas dryer exhaust duct to no more than 35 ft. This length is reduced for each fitting based on the size and type of fitting *(refer to table 12.1 in previous chapter)*. For a dryer exhaust duct that exceeds 35 ft., the installed length must be identified on a permanent tag within 6 ft. of the dryer.

Note: The code permits the installation of a listed dryer exhaust duct power ventilator to increase the length of the dryer duct in accordance with the manufacturer's instructions.

Forced-Air Furnace Return Air/ Outside Air Prohibited Sources

For a forced-air furnace, the code prohibits the following locations as sources of return or outside air:

- Less than 10 ft. from an appliance vent outlet, a plumbing vent, or an exhaust fan outlet, unless the outlet is 3 ft. above the outside air inlet
- Less than 10 ft. above a public way or driveway
- Rooms without an adequate volume of air
- A closet, bathroom, toilet room, kitchen, garage, mechanical room, furnace room, attic, or another dwelling unit
- A crawl space by means of direct connection to the return side of a forced air system
- A room or space containing a non-direct-vent, fuel-burning appliance, unless specific volume and location requirements are met, if that room or space is the sole source of return air

Suspended Unit Heaters

Unless the listing and manufacturer's instructions permit reduced clearances, suspended-type unit heaters must have clearances to combustible materials of at least

- 18 in. from the sides
- 12 in. from the bottom
- 6 in. from the top

Cooking Appliances

The code requires cooking appliances installed in dwelling units to be listed and labeled as household-type appliances for domestic use, or for both domestic and commercial use. The minimum vertical clearance between the cooking surface and combustible materials or metal cabinets above is 30 in. The code permits a clearance of 24 in. for the following:

- Underside of combustible material or metal cabinet covered with ¼ in. insulating millboard covered with sheet metal
- Metal ventilating hood with a ¼ in. space between hood and combustible material or metal cabinet
- Microwave or other cooking appliance listed for 24 in. clearance above cooking surface

14

Plumbing

This chapter covers plumbing system design and installations typical of dwellings. Methods and materials outside the scope of the IRC must comply with the *International Plumbing Code* (IPC).[12]

Water and Sewer Requirements

The water distribution and drainage system of any building must meet the following minimum requirements and be connected to

- An approved public water supply, if available, or individual private water supply such as a well, if the public water supply is not available
- An approved public sewage disposal system or individual private system, such as an on-site septic system, if a public system is not available

General Plumbing Requirements

To perform as intended and to prevent damage or contamination, piping requires adequate support and protection (table 14.1). Concealed piping installed through holes or notches in studs, joists, rafters, or similar members and less than 1¼ in. from the nearest edge of the member requires protection from fastener penetration by shield plates (fig. 14.1).

- Protective shield plates must be at least 0.057-in.-thick (No. 16 gage) steel.
- Plates must cover the area where the pipe passes through the member.
- Shield plates must extend at least 2 in. above sole plates and below the top plates of wall framing.

Note: Cast-iron and galvanized steel pipe do not require protection.

Other general requirements for protection of plumbing piping follow:

- Pipes passing through foundation walls require a pipe sleeve.
- Water, drain, and sewer pipe must be protected from freezing
- Water service pipe is buried at least 12 in. deep and at least 6 in. below the frost line.
- In-ground piping requires continuous support on suitable bedding materials.
- Backfill over pipe must be free of debris, rocks, concrete, and frozen material.

Table 14.1 Piping support

Piping material	Maximum horizontal spacing (ft.)	Maximum vertical spacing (ft.)
ABS pipe	4	10
Cast-iron pipe, < 10 ft. lengths of pipe	5	15
Cast-iron pipe, 10 ft. lengths of pipe	10	15
Copper or copper alloy pipe	12	10
Copper or copper alloy tubing (1¼ in. and smaller)	6	10
Copper or copper alloy tubing (1½ in. and larger)	10	10
Cross-linked polyethylene (PEX) pipe (1 in. and smaller)	2.67	10
Cross-linked polyethylene (PEX) pipe (1¼ in. and larger)	4	10
Cross-linked polyethylene/aluminum/cross-linked polyethylene (PEX-AL-PEX) pipe	2.67	4
CPVC pipe or tubing (1 in. and smaller)	3	10
CPVC pipe or tubing (1¼ in. and larger)	4	10
Polybutylene (PB) pipe or tubing	2.67	4
Polyethylene of raised temperature (PE-RT) pipe (1 in. and smaller)	2.67	10
Polyethylene of raised temperature (PE-RT) pipe (1¼ in. and larger)	4	10
Polypropylene (PP) pipe or tubing (1 in. and smaller)	2.67	10
Polypropylene (PP) pipe or tubing (1¼ in. and larger)	4	10
PVC pipe	4	10
Stainless steel drainage systems	10	10
Steel pipe	12	15

min. 2"

< 1¼"

.057" thick steel plates

min. 2"

Unless it is steel or cast iron piping, plumbing piping installed through studs, plates, joists, and rafters in concealed locations must be protected if less than 1¼" from face of framing.

Figure 14.1 Protection of piping against physical damage

Water Supply System Design Criteria

The system must be designed and installed to deliver adequate water volume and pressure for plumbing fixtures to operate efficiently and properly.

- Approved static pressure for the water service at the building entrance is 40–80 psi.
- Water service pipe must be at least ¾ in.

- Water supply fixture unit values, developed length of piping, and water pressure determine pipe size.

Valves

The IRC prescribes the locations and types of valves required for water distribution systems.

- An accessible main shutoff valve must be located near the entrance of the water service.
- A readily accessible full-open valve is required at each water heater on the cold-water supply pipe.
- An accessible individual shutoff valve is required on the fixture supply pipe to each plumbing fixture other than bathtubs and showers.
- Hose bibbs subject to freezing require an accessible stop-and-waste-type valve inside the building. This valve is not required for frost-proof hose bibbs that extend into heated space.

Water Service Installation

The water service must be protected from potential contamination when installed near the *building sewer*.

- Water service pipe is permitted in the same trench with a building sewer if the sewer pipe is listed for underground use within a building.
- For other types of building sewer pipe, the water service must have at least a 5 ft. horizontal separation or be installed on a ledge at least 12 in. above and to one side of the highest point of the sewer.

Protection of Potable Water Supply from Contamination

To protect the potable water supply, a listed back-flow prevention device is required for the following:

- Hose connections
- Boilers and heat exchangers
- Lawn irrigation systems

An *air gap* is another means to prevent backflow. It is used for the water outlets of fixtures (fig. 14.2). The minimum air gap varies according to fixture type and application (table 14.2).

Table 14.2 Minimum air gaps

Fixture	Minimum air gap	
	Away from a wall (in.)	Close to a wall (in.)
Effective openings greater than 1 in.	Two times the diameter of the effective opening	Three times the diameter of the effective opening
Lavatories and other fixtures with effective opening not greater than ½" in diameter	1	1.5
Over-rim bath fillers and other fixtures with effective openings not greater than 1" in diameter	2	3
Sink, laundry trays, gooseneck back faucets, and other fixtures with effective openings not greater than ¾" in diameter	1.5	2.5

Figure 14.2 Air gap

Source: 2006 International Residential Code Study Companion. Washington, DC: International Code Council, 2006, p. 367.

Dwelling Unit Fire Sprinkler System

The IRC requires an automatic fire sprinkler system in all new one- and two-family dwellings and townhomes. In the plumbing provisions, the code provides a simple, prescriptive approach to the design of dwelling fire sprinkler systems that is an approved alternative to NFPA 13D. The system may be multipurpose—supplying both sprinklers and plumbing fixtures—or a stand-alone system independent of the water distribution system. In either case, a dwelling fire sprinkler system does not require a fire department connection. The code permits any combination of water supply systems to meet the required dwelling fire sprinkler system capacity including the following:

- Domestic water supply
- Well
- Elevated storage tank
- Approved pressure tank
- Stored water source with an automatic pump

Automatic sprinkler protection is not required throughout a one- and two-family dwelling or townhome. Generally, sprinklers are not required in the following areas:

- Closets with areas of 24 sq. ft. or less and not more than 3 ft. deep
- Bathrooms with areas of 55 sq. ft. or less

- Exterior porches
- Garages and carports
- Attics
- Crawl spaces
- Concealed spaces not intended for or used as living spaces

Note: In attics, crawl spaces, and other concealed unoccupied spaces that contain fuel-fired equipment, the code requires a single sprinkler above the equipment.

Non-potable Water Systems

Provisions for collecting, storing, and using various types of non-potable water recognize the growing need for water conservation and the increased implementation of water conservation programs in many regions of the United States. The code addresses the following non-potable water systems:

- Rainwater
- Reclaimed water
- *On-site non-potable water reuse systems*

Note: On-site non-potable water reuse systems include but are not limited to gray water systems. Gray water is the waste from lavatories, bathtubs, showers, washing machines and laundry tubs.

Non-potable water is not safe for drinking, bathing, or cooking purposes, and the code requires clear warning signs at non-potable water outlets such as hose connections and yard hydrants. Other general requirements follow:

- Filtration
- Disinfection as necessary
- Approved storage tanks
- Valves at prescribed locations
- Purple distribution piping
- Piping and storage tank labeling

Non-potable water is typically used for flushing water closets and urinals and for landscape irrigation. The code does not require disinfection of non-potable water used for subsurface landscape irrigation.

Sanitary Drainage

Proper operation of the sanitary drainage system depends on adequate pipe size of approved materials, appropriate slope and support, transition fittings suitable for the location (table 14.3), adequate cleanouts, and proper venting. Total *d.f.u.* of the fixtures served determines pipe sizes (tables 14.4–14.6).

Table 14.3 Fittings for change in direction

	Change in direction		
Type of fitting pattern	**Horizontal to vertical**	**Vertical to horizontal**	**Horizontal to horizontal**
Sixteenth bend	X	X	X
Eighth bend	X	X	X
Sixth bend	X	X	X
Quarter bend	X	X*	X*
Short sweep	X	X*†	X*
Long sweep	X	X	X
Sanitary tee	X	—	—
Wye	X	X	X
Combination wye and eighth bend	X	X	X

*The fittings shall be permitted only for a 2 in. or smaller fixture drain
†3 in. and larger

Table 14.4 Drainage fixture unit (d.f.u.) values for various plumbing fixtures

Type of fixture or group of fixtures	Drainage fixture unit value (d.f.u.)
Bar sink	1
Bathtub (with or without shower head and/or whirlpool attachments)	2
Bidet	1
Clothes washer standpipe	2
Dishwasher	2
Floor drain	0
Kitchen sink	2
Lavatory	1
Laundry tub	2
Shower stall	2
Water closet (1.6 gal. per flush)	3
Water closet (greater than 1.6 gal. per flush)	4
Full-bath group with bathtub (with 1.6 gal. per flush water closet and with or without shower head and/or whirlpool attachment on the bathtub or shower stall)	5
Full-bath group with bathtub (water closet greater than 1.6 gal. per flush, and with or without shower head and/or whirlpool attachment on the bathtub or shower stall)	6
Half-bath group (1.6 gal. per flush water closet plus lavatory)	4
Half-bath group (water closet greater than 1.6 gal. per flush plus lavatory)	5

(continued)

Table 14.4 Drainage fixture unit (d.f.u.) values for various plumbing fixtures (*continued*)

Type of fixture or group of fixtures	Drainage fixture unit value (d.f.u.)
Kitchen group (dishwasher and sink with or without food-waste disposer)	2
Laundry group (clothes washer standpipe and laundry tub)	3
Multiple-bath groups:	
1.5 baths	7
2 baths	8
2.5 baths	9
3 baths	10
3.5 baths	11

Table 14.5 Maximum fixture units allowed to be connected to branches and stacks

Nominal pipe size (in.)	Any horizontal fixture branch	Any one vertical stack or drain
1¼	—	—
1½	3	4
2	6	10
2½	12	20
3	20	48
4	160	240

Note: 1¼ in. pipe is only permitted for a single-fixture drain or trap arm (lavatory). Water closets are not permitted on drain lines less than 3 in.

Table 14.6 Maximum number of fixture units allowed to be connected to building drain, building drain branches, or building sewer

Diameter of pipe (in.)	Slope per ft.		
	⅛ in.	¼ in.	½ in.
2	−	21	27
2½	−	24	31
3	36	42	50
4	180	216	250

Note: Water closets are not permitted on drain lines smaller than 3 in.

Cleanouts

Cleanouts are required in horizontal drain lines at each change of direction greater than 45°. Where more than one change of direction occurs, only one cleanout is required in each 40 ft. A readily removable fixture or trap may serve as a cleanout. Other cleanout requirements follow:

- Cleanouts must have accessible clearance of at least 18 in.
- Cleanouts must allow cleaning in the direction of the flow.
- The required cleanout at the junction of the *building drain* and building sewer may be inside or outside the building. A two-way cleanout is permitted

outside the building to serve both the sewer and the building drain.

Minimum Slope for Horizontal Drainage Piping

The code sets minimum slope requirements for drainage piping based on the pipe size as follows:

- ¼:12 slope for pipe sizes 2½ in. or less
- ⅛:12 slope for pipe sizes 3 in. or more

Vents

Venting provides air to equalize pressure for proper operation of the drainage system, prevents siphoning of water seals, and allows the safe escape of any sewer gas to the outside atmosphere.

- Every trap and trapped fixture must be vented to protect the trap seal.
- At least one vent pipe to the outdoors is required. It must be sized appropriately for the building drain size.

Vent Termination

Proper plumbing vent termination ensures proper operation of the vent, maintains weather resistance of the building, and prevents sewer gas from entering the building.

- Vent pipe termination is at least 6 in. above the roof or 6 in. above the anticipated snow accumulation.
- Vent pipe termination is at least 7 ft. above a roof used for an observation deck or sunbathing deck or for similar purposes.
- Vent extensions through the roof in cold climates that are based on regional outside design temperature require at least 3-in.-diameter pipe, starting 1 ft. inside the building thermal envelope, for protection against frost closure.
- Vents through the roof require approved flashings that are weather tight.
- Minimum clearances from vent terminations to any door, openable window, or other air intake opening are 4 ft. below, 10 ft. horizontally from, or 3 ft. above the opening.

Vent Connections and Grades

The following requirements prevent stoppages and trapping of water in the vent system:

- Vents require adequate slope to allow moisture and condensate to drain back to soil and waste pipes.
- Dry vent connection to a horizontal drain must be above the centerline of the drain.
- Dry vents must to rise vertically to a point at least 6 in. above the flood rim of the fixture.

- Branch vent connection to a vent stack must be at least 6 in. above the flood level of the fixture served.
- If plumbing is roughed in for future fixtures, a vent must be installed to serve those fixtures.

Fixture Vents

Proper slope and maximum lengths for fixture drains ensure proper exchange of air and prevent siphoning of the fixture trap.

- Total fall in a fixture drain to the vent connection cannot exceed one pipe diameter.
- Vent connection to fixture drain is not permitted to be below the trap weir.
- Distance from the trap to the vent is limited as shown in table 14.7, except for self-siphoning fixtures such as water closets (fig. 14.3).

Table 14.7 Maximum distance of fixture trap from vent

Size of trap (in.)	Slope (in. per ft.)	Distance from trap (ft.)
1¼	¼	5
1½	¼	6
2	¼	8
3	¼	12
4	¼	16

Figure 14.3 Trap arm length to vent

Source: 2006 International Residential Code Study Companion. Washington, DC: International Code Council, 2006, p. 389.

Common Vent

A common vent is a single pipe venting two trap arms of fixtures on the same floor, either back to back, or one above the other (table 14.8).

■ Where the drains connect at the same level, the vent connection shall be at the interconnection of the fixture drains or downstream from the interconnection.

■ Where the fixture drains connect at different levels, the upper fixture cannot be a water closet. Vent connection is not permitted upstream from the horizontal drain connections.

Table 14.8 Common vent sizes

Pipe size (in.)	Maximum discharge from upper fixture drain (d.f.u.)
1½	1
2	4
2½ to 3	6

Wet Venting

Vents are required to equalize the pressure in the *DWV* system to preserve the water seal at traps, and to provide air for proper drainage. Wet venting is based on the principle that drain pipe for a fixture or fixtures will have adequate amounts of air to also serve as the vent for a downstream fixture. The section of pipe serving as a wet vent (acting as both a drain and a vent) must be sized adequately and is limited to a lower d.f.u. load than would be allowed for drainage piping (table 14.9).

- Horizontal wet venting is permitted for any combination of fixtures in two bathroom groups.
- Only one fixture is permitted upstream of the dry vent connection to the horizontal wet vent.

Table 14.9 Wet vent size

Wet vent pipe size (in.)	Fixture unit load (d.f.u.)
1½	1
2	4
2½	6
3	12
4	32

■ The dry vent connection to the wet vent must be an individual vent or common vent to any bathroom group fixture except an emergency floor drain.

Waste Stack Vent

A *waste stack* is permitted as a vent for all connected fixtures, provided

■ The waste stack is vertical without offsets between the highest and lowest fixture drain connection.
■ Every fixture drain has a separate connection to the waste stack.
■ The stack does not receive the discharge of water closets or urinals.
■ The *stack vent* is the same size or larger than the waste stack (table 14.10).

Table 14.10 Waste stack vent size

	Maximum number of fixture units (d.f.u.)	
Stack size (in.)	Total discharge into one branch interval	Total discharge for stack
1½	1	2
2	2	4
2½	No limit	8
3	No limit	24
4	No limit	50

Island Fixture Venting

Island venting is an alternative for venting isolated fixtures where other means are not feasible. Island venting must comply with the following:

- Kitchen sinks and lavatories may have island venting (fig. 14.4).
- The fixture vent loops above the level of the sink drain and back down below the floor level before continuing horizontally to a vent.
- The horizontal section is installed as required for drainage piping and is in addition to the fixture drain.
- Cleanouts are required.

Figure 14.4 Island venting

Source: 2006 International Residential Code Study Companion. Washington, DC: International Code Council, 2006, p. 396.

Air Admittance Valves

An air admittance valve is a one-way valve designed to allow air into the plumbing drainage system when a negative pressure develops in the piping (when there is flow from the fixture). The device is at a fixture vent terminal that pulls air from the room in which the fixture is located and is an alternative to venting to the outside air. The valve is designed to close by gravity and seal the terminal under no-flow conditions to prevent introducing sewer gas into the dwelling.

- Approved air admittance valves are permitted for individual, branch, circuit, and stack vents.
- Valves must be installed according to the manufacturer's instructions.
- Installation must be at least 4 in. above branch or fixture drain (fig. 14.5).
- Stack-type air admittance valves must be installed at least 6 in. above the flood-level rim of the highest fixture.
- Air admittance valves installed in attics must be at least 6 in. above insulation.
- The space containing the air admittance valve requires access and ventilation.
- At least one vent is required to extend outdoors to the open air.

Figure 14.5 Air admittance valve

Source: 2006 International Residential Code Study Companion. Washington, DC: International Code Council, 2006, p. 397.

Fixture Traps

Traps provide a water seal to prevent sewer gases from entering the building. Trap sizes vary by fixture (table 14.11). Requirements for fixture traps follow:

- Slip joints must be accessible with a minimum access panel of 12 × 12 in.
- Trap seals must be 2–4 in.
- Floor drains subject to evaporation require *trap-primers* or other approved devices.

Table 14.11 Size of traps and trap arms for plumbing fixtures

Plumbing fixture	Trap size minimum (in.)
Bathtub (with or without shower head and/or whirlpool attachments)	1½
Bidet	1¼
Clothes washer standpipe	2
Dishwasher (on separate trap)	1½
Floor drain	2
Kitchen sink (one or two traps, with or without dishwasher and garbage grinder)	1½
Laundry tub (one or more compartments)	1½
Lavatory	1¼
Shower (based on the total flow rate through showerheads and body sprays) Flow rate:	
5.7 gpm* and less	1½
More than 5.7 gpm up to 12.3 gpm	2
More than 12.3 gpm up to 25.8 gpm	3
More than 25.8 gpm up to 55.6 gpm	4

*gallons per minute

- "S" traps are prohibited.
- Vertical distance from the fixture outlet to the trap weir cannot be more than 24 in.
- Horizontal distance from the fixture outlet to the trap cannot be more than 30 in.

Plumbing Fixtures

Fixtures, faucets, and fixture fittings must have smooth, impervious surfaces and comply with the applicable referenced standards.

Fixture Clearance

Water closets, lavatories, and bidets must meet the following minimum clearance requirements:

- 15 in. from centerline of the fixture to walls or vanities
- 30 in. from centerline to centerline of adjacent fixtures
- 21 in. clearance in front of fixtures

Laundry Standpipes

Standpipes must extend 18–42 in. above the trap weir.

Dishwashers

The IRC sets minimum connection requirements for dishwasher drains to prevent contamination of the dishwasher contents.

- A ¾ in. dishwasher drain may be connected to the sink tailpiece with a *wye fitting* (fig. 14.6).
- The sink, food-waste disposer, and dishwasher may discharge through a single 1½ in. trap.
- The dishwasher waste line must be looped to the underside of the counter as backflow protection.

Figure 14.6 Dishwasher drain

Source: Residential Code Essentials, 2015. Washington, DC: International Code Council, 2015, p. 214.

Showers

The requirements for shower dimensions, access and scald prevention are as follows:

- Shower compartments must be at least 30 × 30 in.
- A minimum width of 25 in. is permitted if the shower area is at least 1,300 sq. in.
- Hinged shower doors must open outward.
- Finished width of at least 22 in. is required for access to shower.
- Shower valves require a water temperature high-limit stop set to no more than 120°F.

Bathtubs and Whirlpool Bathtubs

Bathtubs and whirlpool baths require the following:

- A device to limit water temperature to no more than 120°F
- Access to a circulation pump as follows:
  - Sized and located in accordance with the manufacturer's installation instructions
  - At least 12 × 12 in. or at least 18 × 18 in. if the pump is more than 2 ft. from the access opening
  - An unobstructed access opening large enough to remove the pump

Water Heaters

The IRC prescribes location, installation, and safety requirements for water heaters, including drain pan installations and temperature relief valve provisions.

Required Pan for Water Heaters

If a leaking water heater will cause damage, the water heater must have a pan that meets the following minimum requirements:

- 0.0236 in. galvanized steel, aluminum, or other approved materials
- 1½ in. deep
- ¾ in. indirect waste pipe to approved waste receptor

Note: Safety pan requirements apply to storage-type water heaters, not tankless water heaters.

Pressure and Temperature Relief Valves

Pressure- and temperature-relief valves must

- Not be connected directly to the drainage system
- Discharge to one of the following at a readily observable location:
  - Floor
  - Water heater pan
  - Waste receptor
  - Outdoors

- Terminate not more than 6 in. and not less than two pipe diameters above the floor or approved waste receptor
- Not have valves, tees, traps, or a threaded end

Note: Where PEX or PE-RT tubing is used for discharge piping, the code requires one nominal size larger than the relief-valve outlet with the end of the tubing fastened in place.

Water Heaters Installed in Garages

When a water heater is in a garage, its ignition source must be elevated at least 18 in. above the garage floor (fig. 14.7).

Note: The code does not require elevation of appliances that are listed as flammable vapor ignition-resistant.

Water Heater Seismic Bracing

In SDCs D_0, D_1, and D_2, and for townhomes located in SDC C, water heaters require bracing to resist lateral forces. The code requires anchors or straps in the upper ⅓ and lower ⅓ of the appliance.

gas-fired water heater

gas control

main burner

pilot burner

combustion chamber

18" min.

raised platform

garage floor

Figure 14.7 Water heater elevation in garage

Source: 2006 International Residential Code Study Companion. Washington, DC: International Code Council, 2006, p. 364.

Figure 14.7 Water heater elevation at garage

15

Electrical Systems

The electrical provisions of the IRC are based on the *2020 National Electrical Code* (NEC) (NFPA 70-2020),[13] published by NFPA. Like the IRC, this chapter specifically covers typical electrical installations in constructing one- and two-family dwellings, including

- Services
- Power distribution systems
- Fixtures
- Appliances
- Devices
- Appurtenances

Methods and materials specified in the NEC (NFPA 70) are permitted, even if they are not included in the IRC. However, electrical systems or components not specifically covered in the IRC must comply with the applicable provisions of the NEC (NFPA 70).

Scope

The scope of the IRC covers single-phase services that are not more than 120/240-volt and 400 *amps*.

Equipment Location and Clearances

Following are the minimum requirements for service equipment (i.e., service panel or subpanel):

- Working space in front of equipment is at least 30 in. wide × 36 in. deep.
- Headroom for working spaces for service equipment and panelboards is at least 6 ft. 6 in.
- Illumination is provided.
- Working space must not be storage space.
- Panelboards must not be in clothes closets or bathrooms.
- Dedicated space above and below panels equals the width of panel from floor to structural ceiling (fig. 15.1).

Minimum Size of Conductors

The minimum sizes of conductors for feeders and branch circuits are 14 AWG copper and 12 AWG aluminum.

Figure 15.1 Service working space and clearances

Conductor and Terminal Identification

Device terminals other than panelboards and certain devices rated over 30 amps require properly identified terminals.

Grounded (Neutral) Conductors and Terminals

The requirements for identifying *grounded conductors* and terminals are as follows:

- Grounded conductors not more than 6 AWG are identified by white or gray insulation, or bear three white stripes on other than green insulated wire.
- Grounded conductors greater than 6 AWG are white or gray, or bear three white stripes on other than green insulation, or have white or gray tape applied to terminal ends at installation.
- Receptacles and polarized attachment plugs require the grounded terminal to be identified in one of three ways as follows:
  - Substantially white in color
  - Bear the word "white"
  - Bear the letter "W"

Grounding Conductors

Identification of *grounding conductors* must comply
with the following:

- Grounding conductors not more than 6 AWG
  are green or green with yellow stripes when not
  bare wire.
- Grounding conductors greater than 6 AWG have
  green insulation or yellow stripes on green insulation, or are bare wires. If the insulation is another
  color, the electrician may mark the conductors
  with green tape or permanent marking (or strip
  insulation to bare wire) at terminal ends and access
  points at the time of installation.

Ungrounded (Hot) Conductors

Ungrounded conductors must be identified as follows:

- Ungrounded conductors are any color other than
  white, gray, or green.
- White, gray, or green insulated conductors in
  cable or flexible cord assemblies or switch loops
  may be used as ungrounded conductors if they are
  re-identified with permanent markings.

Electrical Services

The electrical service is typically a panelboard with a main disconnect that shuts off all power to the building, the circuit breakers serving the branch circuits, and related equipment. The serving utility company delivers electrical power to the service entrance conductors, which in turn conduct the energy to the main service disconnect. The service distributes electricity to the premises wiring system.

■ Only one service is permitted for one- and two-family dwellings.

■ Service conductors supplying a building are not permitted to pass through the interior of another building.

■ Only service conductors are permitted in the same service raceway or service cable.

■ A service disconnect must be installed at a readily accessible location either outside of a building or inside, near to where the service conductors enter the building.

■ Service disconnects are not permitted in bathrooms.

■ Occupants must have access to the disconnect that serves their dwelling unit.

■ A surge-protective device (SPD) is required at the service panel.

Electrical Service Size and Rating

The minimum service rating for single-family dwellings is 100 amps (60 amps for other installations). The *ampacity* of ungrounded service conductors and the rating of the service disconnect may not be less than the load served. Table 15.1 contains the formulas to calculate the minimum service load for a single-family dwelling.

Emergency Disconnect

The code requires an emergency disconnect at a readily accessible location outside the building (fig. 15.2).

- The outside emergency disconnect can also serve as the service disconnect.
- A sign or marker is required with text matching the wording specified by the code.
- The sign or marking must indicate that the device is an emergency disconnect and whether it also serves as a meter disconnect or service disconnect.

Table 15.1 Minimum service load calculation for single-family dwellings

Loads and procedure			Volt-amperes
1. General lighting and general use receptacle outlets	3 volt-amperes	× _____ Floor area (sq. ft.)	_____ VA
		Plus	
2. All 20-ampere-rated small appliance and laundry circuits	1,500 volt-amperes	× _____ Number of circuits	_____ VA
		Plus	
3. Appliances	The nameplate volt-ampere rating of all permanent or dedicated appliances:		
	Ranges		_____ VA
	Ovens		_____ VA
	Cooking units		_____ VA
	Clothes dryers		_____ VA
	Water heaters		_____ VA
	Subtotal		_____ **VA**

(continued)

Table 15.1 Minimum service load calculation for single-family dwellings *(continued)*

Loads and procedure			Volt-amperes
4. Apply the following demand factors to the above subtotal:	100%	× First 10,000 volt-amperes	**Plus** ____ VA
	40%	× Portion in excess of 10,000 volt-amperes	**Plus** ____ VA
5. Air-conditioning		Total of the nameplate rating(s) of the air-conditioning and cooling equipment	**Plus** ____ VA
		Total volt-amperes	____ VA
Total load in amperes	**Volt-ampere sum**	÷ 240 volts =	**AMPS**

Meter

Emergency disconnect

EMERGENCY DISCONNECT

NOT SERVICE EQUIPMENT

Required marking

Ungrounded service conductors

Service disconnect

Grounded (neutral) conductor

Main bonding jumper

Grounding conductor terminals

Figure 15.2 Emergency disconnect required at readily accessible outdoor location

Service Conductor Size

The IRC requires the following sizing of service conductors:

- Ungrounded (hot phase leg) service conductors must have a minimum size as identified in table 15.2.
- The grounded (neutral) conductor ampacity must be at least the maximum unbalance of the load. Its size must be at least the required minimum *grounding electrode conductor* size.
- The grounding electrode conductors are sized based on the size of the service entrance conductors (table 15.2).

Overhead Service-Drop and Service-Conductor Installation

The code prescribes the following minimum clearance requirements for overhead services:

- Open conductors require at least a 3 ft. horizontal separation from openings and porches and at least 3 ft. below openable windows.
- Vertical clearance height is as follows:
  - At least 3 ft. above roofs with a pitch of at least 4:12
  - At least 8 ft. above roofs with a pitch of less than 4:12
  - At least 18 in. over 4 ft. of roof overhang

Table 15.2 Service conductor and grounding electrode

Conductor types and sizes—THHN, THHW, THW, THWN, USE, XHHW, THW-2, THWN-2, XHHW-2, SE, USE-2		Allowable ampacity	Minimum grounding electrode conductor size	
Copper (AWG)	Aluminum and copper-clad aluminum (AWG)	Maximum load (amps)	Copper (AWG)	Aluminum (AWG)
4	2	100	8	6
3	1	110	8	6
2	1/0	125	8	6
1	2/0	150	6	4
1/0	3/0	175	6	4
2/0	4/0 or two sets of 1/0	200	4	2
3/0	250 kcmil or two sets of 2/0	225	4	2
4/0 or two sets of 1/0	300 kcmil or two sets of 3/0	250	2	1/0
250 kcmil or two sets of 2/0	350 kcmil or two sets of 4/0	300	2	1/0
350 kcmil or two sets of 3/0	500 kcmil or two sets of 250 kcmil	350	2	1/0
400 kcmil or two sets of 4/0	600 kcmil or two sets of 300 kcmil	400	1/0	3/0

Note: Service conductors in parallel sets of 1/0 and larger are permitted in either a single raceway or in separate raceways. Grounding electrode conductors of size 8 AWG require protection with conduit. Grounding electrode conductors of size 6 AWG require protection with conduit or must closely follow a structural surface for physical protection.

- At least 10 ft. over grade, sidewalks, and walking surfaces at service entrance point and below drip loop
- At least 12 ft. over driveways and residential property

System Grounding and Bonding

The grounding system provides a fault current path to earth. The code provides for bonding of metal parts that have potential to become energized to provide an effective path for fault current.

■ System (including service equipment enclosures, *equipment grounding conductors,* and grounded service conductor) is grounded at service with grounding electrode conductor connected to grounding electrode system.

■ A main *bonding jumper* (such as the green machine screw or green insulated conductor supplied with the service enclosure) is required to connect the equipment grounding conductors to the service equipment enclosure and the grounded (neutral) conductors.

Grounding Electrode System

The following electrodes, if available, are bonded together to form the grounding electrode system:

- Underground metal water pipe with at least 10 ft. in contact with the ground (must be supplemented by another type of electrode)
- 20 ft. of ½ in. reinforcing bar or 20 ft. of 4 AWG bare copper wire encased in concrete footing/ foundation that is in contact with the ground
- Ground ring at least 30 in. below ground and at least 20 ft. of 2 AWG bare copper wire
- Plate electrode at least 2 sq. ft. and at least 30 in. below ground
- Listed copper clad ground rod, ⅝ in. diameter × 8 ft. long (or other approved pipe or rod electrode) *Note: Where ground rods are installed, at least two are required unless resistance testing indicates otherwise. A minimum separation distance of 6 ft. is required.*

Bonding

The code provides for the bonding of metal parts associated with the electrical system to provide an effective path for fault current.

- *Bonding* is required to ensure electrical continuity of the grounding system at service equipment, raceways, and enclosures.

- Bonding of the metal water piping system to the service equipment enclosure (or other approved location) with an appropriately sized bonding conductor is required to provide a fault path, in case the water pipe becomes energized through accidental contact with hot wires. The water piping system is not a ground or *grounding electrode.* The points of attachment of the bonding jumper must be accessible.
- For bonding of other systems—typically telephone, satellite and cable television systems—to the building grounding system, the code requires installation of an intersystem bonding termination near the building service equipment with a capacity for at least 3 bonding conductors.

Grounding Electrode Conductors

Grounding electrode conductors connect the electrical grounding system to the grounding electrodes. The following requirements apply:

- Grounding electrode conductors may not be spliced except by an approved irreversible process.
- Grounding electrode conductors require protection (such as approved conduit) if exposed to potential physical damage.
- Connections to electrodes require approved fittings to ensure an effective grounding path.

Branch Circuit Ratings

Branch circuits must be rated according to the maximum allowable ampere rating or setting of the *overcurrent protection device* (table 15.3). The ampere rating or setting of the specified overcurrent device determines the circuit rating for conductors of higher ampacity.

Table 15.3 Branch-circuit requirement

	Circuit rating		
	15 amp	20 amp	30 amp

Conductors:
    Minimum size (AWG) circuit
    conductors (copper)
	14	12	10

Overcurrent-protection device: maximum ampere rating	15	20	30
Outlet receptacle rating (amperes)	15 maximum	15 or 20	30
Maximum load (amperes)	15	20	30

Required Branch Circuits

The IRC requires the following branch circuits:

■ Central heating equipment requires an individual branch circuit.

■ Kitchen countertop receptacles require at least two, 20 amp-rated branch circuits. These circuits also are permitted to supply other receptacle outlets in the kitchen, pantry, breakfast, and dining areas, including the outlet for the refrigerator.

■ Receptacle outlets serving the refrigerator, dishwasher or other appliances are permitted on individual branch circuits rated 15 amps.

■ The code requires a separate 20-amp laundry circuit to serve all laundry area receptacles.

■ Required bathroom receptacle outlet(s) require at least one 20 amp circuit that serves no other outlets.

• The code permits the circuit to supply other equipment in the bathroom, such as a light or fan, if the circuit is dedicated to one bathroom.

■ A separate 20-amp branch circuit is required for required receptacle outlets in an attached garage or a detached garage with electrical power.

• This circuit is permitted to supply readily accessible outdoor receptacle outlets

Conductor Sizing and Overcurrent Protection

Table 15.4 lists ampacities for conductors. Note the following:

■ The temperature rating of the conductor insulation must be suitable for the device or location.

Table 15.4 Allowable ampacities

Conductor size	Conductor temperature rating		
	60°C	75°C	90°C
	Types	Types	Types
	TW, UF	RHW, THHW, THW, THWN, USE, XHHW	RHW-2, THHN, THHW, THW-2, THWN-2, XHHW, XHHW-2, USE-2
AWG kcmil	Copper		
18	–	–	14
16	–	–	18
14	20	20	25
12	25	25	30
10	30	35	40
8	40	50	55
6	55	65	75
4	70	85	95
3	85	100	110
2	95	115	130
1	110	130	150
1/0	125	150	170
2/0	145	175	195
3/0	165	200	225
4/0	195	230	260

Table 15.4 Allowable ampacities (*continued*)

Conductor size	Conductor temperature rating		
	60°C	**75°C**	**90°C**
	Types	**Types**	**Types**
AWG kcmil	TW, UF	RHW, THHW, THW, THWN, USE, XHHW	RHW-2, THHN, THHW, THW-2, THWN-2, XHHW, XHHW-2, USE-2
	Aluminum or copper-clad aluminum		
18	–	–	–
16	–	–	–
14	–	–	–
12	20	20	25
10	25	30	35
8	30	40	45
6	40	50	60
4	55	65	75
3	65	75	85
2	75	90	100
1	85	100	115
1/0	100	120	135
2/0	115	135	150
3/0	130	155	175
4/0	150	180	205

- When conductors are bundled or stacked or there are more than three current-carrying conductors in a cable or raceway greater than 24 in. long, ampacity ratings are reduced (table 15.5).
- The temperature rating of the terminal must be considered in calculating the ampacity of the conductor.

Overcurrent Protection Required

An overcurrent device, such as a circuit breaker, must protect all ungrounded branch-circuit and feeder conductors. Overcurrent protective device ratings or settings may not exceed the allowable ampacity of the conductor (table 15.6).

Location of Overcurrent Devices

Overcurrent devices must be
- Readily accessible
- Not subject to damage
- Not in clothes closets or bathrooms
- Not located over steps
- Not more than 6 ft. 7 in. above floor

Table 15.5 Conductor proximity adjustment factors

Number of current-carrying conductors in cable or raceway	% of values in allowable ampacities table
4–6	80
7–9	70
10–20	50
21–30	45
31–40	40
41 and above	35

Table 15.6 Overcurrent protection rating

Copper		Aluminum or copper-clad aluminum	
Size (AWG)	Maximum overcurrent protection device rating (amps)	Size (AWG)	Maximum overcurrent protection device rating (amps)
14	15	12	15
12	20	10	25
10	30	8	30

Note: The maximum overcurrent protection device rating shall not exceed the conductor's allowable ampacity after applying any correction or adjustment factors.

Wiring Methods

The IRC recognizes a number of approved wiring methods, including armored cable, metal-clad cable, and conductors installed in various types of metallic and nonmetallic conduit. Unless stated otherwise, this section generally refers to aboveground wiring methods using nonmetallic (type NM) sheathed cable common to one- and two-family dwelling and townhome construction (table 15.7). The cable must be approved for the location. For example, type NM cable is not permitted underground, may not be used in wet or damp locations, and is not to be embedded in concrete. Other wiring methods are permitted in accordance with the code.

- Cables in accessible attics with permanent stairs require protection when installed as follows:
  - Across the tops of joists
  - On the faces of studs within 7 ft. above the floor joists
  - On the faces of rafters within 7 ft. above the floor joists
- Cables in accessible attics without permanent stairs must be protected only if they are within 6 ft. of the attic entrance.

Table 15.7 Installation requirements for nonmetallic sheathed cable

Installation	Physical protection	
	Minimum setback from edge of framing (in.)	Physical protection if minimum distance is not met
Cable run parallel with the framing member or furring strip	1¼ in.	0.0625-in. steel plate or sleeve
Cable in bored holes or notches in framing members	1¼ in.	0.0625-in. steel plate or sleeve
Cable installed in grooves and covered	1¼ in. free space	0.0625 in. steel plate or sleeve
Securely fastened bushings or grommets are required to protect cable run through openings in metal framing members	—	—
	Support of cable	
Maximum allowable on center support spacing	4.5 ft.	
Maximum support distance from metal box with cable clamp	12 in.	
Maximum support distance from plastic box without cable clamp	8 in.	
Flat cables shall not be stapled on edge	—	

- Exposed cable must
  - Closely follow the surface of the building finish or running boards
  - Be protected from physical damage
  - Have a sunlight-resistant listing if exposed to sunlight
- Unfinished basements with type SE or NM cable that runs at angles with joists must adhere to the following requirements:
  - Cables with two or more conductors at least 6 AWG may be attached directly to the bottom of joists.
  - Cables with three or more conductors at least 8 AWG may be attached directly to the bottom of joists.
  - Smaller cables must run either through bored holes in joists or on running boards.

Note: For wall installations in unfinished basements, Type NM cable installed in a listed conduit or tubing satisfies the physical protection requirement.

Underground Installation Requirements

Cable installed underground must be listed and labeled for the location. In addition, direct burial conductors and cables emerging from the ground must be protected from 18 in. below grade to 8 ft. above grade (table 15.8). Direct burial conductors

Table 15.8 Minimum cover requirements, burial (in.)

Location of wiring method or circuit	Type of wiring method or circuit	
	Direct burial cables or conductors	Rigid metal conduit or intermediate metal conduit
All locations not specified below	24	6
In trench below 2-in.-thick concrete or equivalent	18	6
Under a building	0 (in raceway only)	0
Under minimum of 4-in.- thick concrete exterior slab with no vehicular traffic and the slab extending not less than 6 in. beyond the underground installation	18	4
Under streets, highways, roads, alleys, driveways and parking lots	24	24
One- and two-family dwelling driveways and outdoor parking areas, and used only for dwelling-related purposes	18	18
In solid rock where covered by minimum of 2 in. concrete extending down to rock	2 (in raceway only)	2

Table 15.8 Minimum cover requirements, burial (in.) (*continued*)

Type of wiring method or circuit		
Nonmetallic raceways listed for direct burial without concrete encasement or other approved raceways	Residential branch circuits rated 120 volts or less with GFCI protection and maximum overcurrent protection of 20 amperes	Circuits for control of irrigation and landscape lighting limited to not more than 30 volts and installed with type UF or in other identified cable or raceway
18	12	6
12	6	6
0	0 (in raceway only)	0 (in raceway only)
4	6 (direct burial) 4 (in raceway)	6 (direct burial) 4 (in raceway)
24	24	24
18	12	18
2	2 (in raceway only)	2 (in raceway only)

emerging from the ground and subject to physical damage require one of the following for protection:

- Rigid metal conduit
- Intermediate metal conduit
- Schedule 80 PVC conduit

Note: Splices underground are permitted only with specific approved methods and listed materials.

General Purpose Receptacle Distribution

In addition to providing convenience for the occupants, proper placement of receptacle outlets to serve fixtures and appliances can reduce electrical hazards in the home that may occur with the use of extension cords. The IRC provides minimum distribution requirements for general purpose receptacle outlets rated at 125 volts, 15 and 20 amps.

Habitable Rooms

Any point along a wall must be within 6 ft. of a receptacle outlet (fig. 15.3).

Kitchen Counters

The location requirements for receptacle outlets serving kitchen counters are as follows:

- Any point along a kitchen wall counter must be within 2 ft. of a receptacle outlet (fig. 15.4).

Figure 15.3 Receptacle outlet locations

Source: 2006 International Residential Code Study Companion. Washington, DC: International Code Council, 2006, p. 438.

- At least one receptacle outlet is provided for the first 9 sq. ft. of island and peninsular counters and one outlet for each additional 18 sq. ft.
- One receptacle outlet is located within 2 ft. of the end of peninsular counters.
- Required receptacles may be no higher than 20 in. above counter.
- Receptacles are permitted 12 in. or less below counters.

Figure 15.4 Kitchen counter receptacle outlet locations

Source: 2006 International Residential Code Study Companion. Washington, DC: International Code Council, 2006, p. 439.

Bathroom
A receptacle outlet is required within 36 in. of each lavatory.

Outdoors
A receptacle outlet no more than 6 ft. 6 in. above grade or walking surface is required at each of the following locations:
- Front of dwelling unit
- Back of dwelling unit
- Each balcony, deck, or porch that is accessed from inside the dwelling unit

Laundry Areas
At least one outlet is required for laundry appliances.

Basements, Garages, and Accessory Buildings
Basements, garages, and accessory buildings require receptacle outlets as follows:
- Each separate unfinished portion of a basement requires at least one receptacle outlet.
- Attached garages and detached garages with electrical power require at least one receptacle outlet located in each vehicle space.
- Detached accessory buildings with electrical power require at least one receptacle outlet.

Hallways

The code requires at least one receptacle outlet in hallways 10 ft. or longer.

Foyers

For foyers greater than 60 sq. ft., the code requires a receptacle outlet for each wall space 3 ft. or greater in width.

HVAC Equipment

A receptacle outlet is required within 25 ft. of HVAC equipment for service of the equipment.

Ground-Fault Circuit Interrupter (GFCI) Protection

Single-phase 125-volt through 250 volt receptacle outlets at the following locations require GFCI protection:

- Bathrooms
- Garages and accessory buildings
- Outdoors
- Crawl spaces including lighting outlets
- Basements
- Kitchen receptacles serving countertops
- Indoor damp and wet location
- Within 6 ft. of sinks, including laundry, utility, and bar sinks

- Within 6 feet of the outside edge of a bathtub or shower stall
- Laundry areas
- Kitchen dishwasher branch circuit
- Indoor damp and wet locations

Note: Receptacle outlets located in basements and serving permanently installed burglar or fire alarm systems do not require GFCI protection.

Note: GFCI devices must be readily accessible and cannot be installed behind appliances such as refrigerators.

Arc-Fault Circuit Interrupter (AFCI) Protection

AFCIs detect unwanted arcing in the wiring of the branch circuit and open the circuit before excessive heat buildup can cause a fire. Typically, a combination-type arc-fault circuit breaker protecting the entire branch circuit satisfies this requirement, but the code does offer other options. AFCIs are required for branch circuits supplying 120-volt, single-phase, 15- and 20-amp outlets, including receptacle, lighting and smoke alarm outlets, installed in the following locations and similar rooms or areas:

- Bedrooms
- Closets
- Dens
- Dining rooms

- Family rooms
- Hallways
- Kitchens
- Laundry areas
- Living rooms
- Libraries
- Parlors
- Recreation rooms
- Sunrooms

Lighting Outlets

Wall-switch-controlled lighting outlets are required at the following locations:

- Habitable rooms
  Note: Switch-controlled receptacle outlets satisfy the requirement in habitable rooms, except in kitchens.
- Bathrooms
- Stairways
  Note: Switches must be located at each level when the stair has six or more risers.
- Outside each exterior door with grade-level access
- Hallways
- Attached garages and detached garages with power
- Storage and equipment spaces, including attics

Boxes

A box is required at each splice, junction, outlet, switch, and pull point. Following are other requirements for boxes:

- All metal boxes require grounding by approved means.
- Type NM cable must extend into a nonmetallic box at least ¼ in. and be anchored within 8 in. of the box.
- The sheath of Type NM cable must extend into a metallic box at least ¼ in. and beyond the cable clamp.
- Boxes supporting luminaires that weigh more than 50 lb. must be listed and marked for the purpose.
- Boxes that support ceiling paddle fans must be listed and marked for the purpose and, when designed to support more than 35 lb., must state the maximum weight.
- Boxes may not support ceiling paddle fans weighing more than 70 lb.
- Each box is limited to a maximum box fill capacity based on the size of the box, the number and size of conductors entering the box, and the devices and fit- tings installed.
- Unused openings must be closed by approved methods.

- Boxes may be set back no more than ¼ in. from noncombustible finishes such as ceramic tile and concrete.
- Boxes must be flush with or project in front of combustible finish surfaces such as wood and drywall.

Note: Nonmetallic-sheathed cable entering nonmetallic boxes not larger than 2¼ by 4 in. does not need to be secured to the box.

Receptacles

The code requires the following for installation of receptacle devices:

- A single receptacle installed on an individual branch circuit must have an ampere rating not less than that of the branch circuit.
- Receptacles connected to a branch circuit supplying two or more receptacles require an amp rating as specified in table 15.3.
- Receptacles of 15 and 20 amps installed in a wet location, whether in use (with a cord plugged in) or not, require enclosures, such as bubble covers, that are weatherproof.
- The code prohibits receptacles within or directly over a bathtub or shower space or less than 36 in. horizontally from a bathtub or shower.

Tamper-Resistant Receptacles

In general, the code requires tamper-resistant receptacles for all 125 volt, 15 and 20 amp receptacles associated with dwelling units and garages.

The following applications do not require tamper-resistant receptacles:

- Receptacles located more than 5.5 ft. above the floor.
- Receptacles that are part of a luminaire or appliance.
- A single receptacle for a single appliance or a duplex receptacle for two appliances where located in dedicated space behind the appliance.
- Receptacles in accessory buildings that are not garages
- Receptacles in attics and crawl spaces

Fixtures

The code regulates electrical fixtures for type, location, and clearance to combustibles.

Bathtub and Shower Areas

Specific requirements apply for fixture installations in a zone measured 3 ft. horizontally and 8 ft. vertically from the top of a bathtub rim or shower stall threshold as follows:

- Cord-connected or suspended luminaires, track lighting, pendants, and ceiling-suspended (paddle) fans are prohibited.
- Luminaires must be listed for damp locations.
- Luminaires subject to shower spray must be listed for wet locations.

Luminaires in Clothes Closets

To reduce fire hazard, the code restricts luminaires adjacent to storage areas of clothes closets. The storage area comprises the following space:

- Within 24 in. of the side and back walls and the greater of 6 ft. high or to the highest rod
- The space above 6 ft. that is within 12 in. (or the shelf width, if greater) of the side and back walls

Permitted Luminaires

The following types of luminaires are permitted in clothes closets:

- Surface-mounted or recessed incandescent, with completely enclosed lamps
- Surface-mounted or recessed fluorescent
- LED luminaires

Prohibited Luminaires

The following types of luminaires are prohibited in clothes closets:

- Incandescent luminaires with open or partially enclosed lamps
- Pendant luminaires
- Lamp holders

Luminaire Installation and Clearances in Clothes Closets

Luminaires typically must be installed on or recessed into the ceiling or the wall above the door. Specified clearances are measured from the fixture to the nearest point of the defined storage space (fig. 15.5). Minimum clearances are as follows:

- At least 12 in. for surface-mounted incandescent and LED luminaires
- At least 6 in. for recessed incandescent and LED luminaires with a completely enclosed lamp
- At least 6 in. for surface-mounted and recessed fluorescent luminaires

Note: *When specifically identified as suitable for installation within the closet storage space, both surface mounted LED luminaires and surface mounted fluorescent luminaires may be installed anywhere in a clothes closet in accordance with the manufacturer's installation instructions.*

Figure 15.5 Luminaires in clothes closets

Note: Surface-mounted fluorescent or LED luminaries identified as suitable for storage space are permitted anywhere in a clothes closet when installed according to the manufacturer's instructions.

Recessed Luminaire Installation and Clearance

The IRC prescribes the following clearances for recessed luminaires:

- All recessed parts must be at least ½ in. from combustible materials, unless the luminaire is identified for contact with insulation (Type IC).
- Thermal insulation cannot be installed above a recessed luminaire or within 3 in. of the recessed luminaire unless the luminaire is identified for contact with insulation (Type IC).

Epilogue

Communication between the builder and the local building department is essential to completing construction correctly, on schedule, and within budget. In addition to providing information on local amendments and regional design criteria, the local authority is responsible for interpreting the code and establishing administrative procedures for permits, inspections, testing, appeals, and certificates of occupancy.

Home Builders' Jobsite Codes has been developed as an accurate, abbreviated guide to the frequently used provisions of the *International Residential Code (IRC).* To protect public health, safety, and welfare, the IRC sets minimum requirements for the construction of one- and two-family dwellings and townhomes. It is a comprehensive residential code that emphasizes prescriptive methods—specific lists of rules the home builder may follow to comply with the code.

Notes

[1] *2018 International Building Code.* Washington, DC: International Code Council, Inc., 2014.

[2] *ASCE/SEI 7 (2010) Minimum Design Loads for Buildings and Other Structures with Supplement No. 1.* Reston, VA: American Society of Civil Engineers, Structural Engineering Institute, 2010.

[3] *ICC 600 (2014) Standard for Residential Construction in High-wind Regions.* Washington, DC: International Code Council, Inc., 2014.

[4] *Wood Frame Construction Manual for One- and Two-family Dwellings (AWC WFCM—2015).* Leesburg, VA: American Wood Council, 2015.

[5] *ICC 500 (2014) Standard on the Design and Construction of Storm Shelters.* Washington, DC: International Code Council, Inc., 2014.

[6]*NFPA 13D (2013) Standard for the Installation of Sprinkler Systems in One- and Two-family Dwellings and Manufactured Homes.* Quincy, MA: National Fire Protection Association, 2012.

[7]*2018 International Energy Conservation Code.* Washington, DC: International Code Council, Inc., 2014.

[8]*2018 International Mechanical Code.* Washington, DC: International Code Council, Inc., 2014.

[9]*2018 International Fuel Gas Code.* Washington, DC: International Code Council, Inc., 2014.

[10]*NFPA 31 (2011) Standard for the Installation of Oil- burning Equipment.* Quincy, MA.: National Fire Protection Association, 2011.

[11]*2018 International Fuel Gas Code.* Washington, DC: International Code Council, Inc., 2014.

[12]*2018 International Plumbing Code.* Washington, DC: International Code Council, Inc., 2014.

[13]*NFPA 70 (2017) National Electrical Code.* Quincy, MA.: National Fire Protection Association, 2013.

Glossary

access (to) (accessible). That which enables a device, an appliance or equipment to be reached by ready access or by a means that first requires the removal or movement of a panel, door or similar obstruction.

accessory structure. A building, such as a detached garage or shed, that is accessory to and incidental to that of the dwelling, and located on the same lot as the dwelling.

AFCI. Arc-fault circuit interrupter, a device that detects unwanted arcing in the wiring of the branch circuit and opens the circuit before excessive heat buildup can cause a fire.

air gap. Open space between the potable water outlet and the flood-level rim of the fixture, designed to separate the potable water from the source of contamination.

air-impermeable insulation. An insulation having an air permeance equal to or less than 0.02 L/s-m^2 at 75 Pa pressure differential when tested according to ASTM E 2178 or E 283.

ampacity. The current, in amperes, that a conductor can carry continuously under the conditions of use without exceeding its temperature rating.

amps. Amperes, a measurement of electrical current.

attic. The unfinished space between the ceiling assembly and the roof assembly

AWG. American Wire Gage. The term indicates the size of the wire. As the AWG number decreases, the wire diameter increases.

balanced ventilation system. A ventilation system where the total supply airflow and total exhaust airflow are simultaneously within 10 percent of their averages.

bathroom. A room containing a bathtub, shower, spa, or similar bathing fixture.

bonding. Permanent joining of metallic parts to form an electrically conductive path that will ensure electrical continuity and the capacity to conduct safely any current likely to be imposed. Bonding is not the same as grounding, although the two terms are sometimes confused.

bonding jumper. A reliable conductor to ensure the required electrical conductivity between metal parts required to be electrically connected.

braced wall line. A straight line through the building plan that represents the location of the lateral resistance provided by the wall bracing.

braced wall line, continuously sheathed. A braced wall line with structural sheathing applied to all sheathable surfaces including the areas above and below openings.

braced wall panel. A full-height section of wall constructed to resist in-plane shear loads through interaction of framing members, sheathing material, and anchors. The panel's length meets the requirements of its particular bracing method, and contributes toward the total amount of bracing required along its braced wall line.

Btu/h. British thermal units per hour.

building drain. Lowest drainage piping inside the house; extends 30 in. beyond the exterior walls to connect to the building sewer. The building drain collects the discharge from all other drainage piping in the dwelling.

building sewer. That part of the drainage system that begins 30 in. outside of the building, at the end of the building drain, and conveys its discharge to a public sewer, private sewer, individual sewage disposal system, or other approved point of disposal.

Category IV appliance. An appliance that operates with a positive vent static pressure and with a vent gas temperature that is capable of causing excessive condensate production in the vent. Category IV appliances are referred to as very high efficiency condensing appliances. They rely on mechanical means rather than gravity to vent the low temperature flue gases to the outside. Vents must be noncorrosive material, such as PVC pipe, or as specified by the appliance manufacturer.

cfm. Cubic feet per minute.

cricket. A sloped flashing on the up-roof side of a chimney to divert water from above the chimney to each side.

dead loads. Weight of all materials of construction incorporated into the building, including but not limited to walls, floors, roofs, ceilings, stairways, built-in partitions, finishes, cladding, and fixed-service equipment. Dead loads are permanent.

d.f.u. In plumbing, drainage fixture units, a measurement of probable discharge into the drainage system by various types of plumbing fixtures, used to size DWV piping systems.

DWV. In plumbing, the drainage, waste, and vent system. It consists of all pipes that convey wastes from plumbing fixtures, appliances, and appurtenances, including fixture traps, above-grade drainage piping, below-grade drains within the building, below- and above-grade venting systems, and piping to the public sewer or private septic system.

direct-vent appliance. Fuel-burning appliance with a sealed combustion system that draws all air for combustion from the outside atmosphere and discharges all flue gases to the outside atmosphere.

dwelling. A building that contains one or two dwelling units occupied or intended to be occupied for living purposes.

dwelling unit. A single unit providing complete independent living facilities for one or more persons, including permanent provisions for living, sleeping, eating, cooking, and sanitation.

emergency escape and rescue opening. An operable exterior window, door or other similar device that provides for a means of escape and access for rescue in the event of an emergency.

equipment grounding conductor. Conductor used to connect the noncurrent-carrying metal parts of equipment, conduit, and other enclosures to the system-grounded (neutral) conductor, the grounding electrode conductor, or both, at the service equipment.

fenestration. Skylights, roof windows, vertical windows (whether fixed or moveable); opaque doors; glazed doors; glass block; and combination opaque/glazed doors.

flashover. The sudden and rapid spread of fire caused by the near-simultaneous ignition of all combustible smoke, fumes, and exposed materials in an enclosed space.

flight. A continuous run of stair treads between landings.

footcandle. A unit of measure of the intensity of light falling on a surface, equal to one lumen per square foot and originally defined with reference to a standardized candle burning at one foot from a given surface.

GFCI. Ground-fault circuit interrupter. A device intended to protect people, it functions to de-energize a circuit within an established period of time when a current to ground exceeds a certain value (indicating a fault).

grade floor emergency escape and rescue opening. An emergency escape and rescue opening located such that the bottom of the clear opening is not more than 44 inches above or below the finished ground level adjacent to the opening.

grade plane. A reference plane representing the average of the finished ground level adjoining the building at all exterior walls. Where the finished ground level slopes away from the exterior walls, the grade plane is established by the lowest points within the area between the building and the lot line. Where the lot line is more than 6 ft. from the building the grade plane is established by the lowest points between the structure and a point 6 ft. from the building.

gray water. Waste discharged from lavatories, bathtubs, showers, clothes washers and laundry trays.

grounded conductor. System or circuit conductor that is intentionally grounded. This is commonly referred to as the neutral and is sometimes confused with the terminology for grounding conductor. Grounded conductors (wires) generally are marked with white.

grounding conductor. A conductor used to connect equipment, or the grounded circuit of a wiring system to a grounding electrode or electrodes. The grounding conductor typically bonds to the grounded (neutral) conductor at the service equipment only and typically has green markings or is bare wire.

grounding electrode. Device that establishes an electrical connection to earth. Ground rods and underground copper water service piping are examples of grounding electrodes.

grounding electrode conductor. Conductor used to connect the grounding electrode(s) to the equipment grounding conductor, to the grounded conductor, or to both, typically at the service.

habitable attic. A finished or unfinished habitable space within an attic.

habitable space. Space in a building for living, sleeping, eating, or cooking. Bathrooms, toilet rooms, closets, halls, storage or utility spaces, and similar areas are not considered habitable spaces.

high-efficacy light sources. Any lamp with an efficacy of not less than 65 lumens per watt, or luminaires with an efficacy of not less than 45 lumens per watt.

interlayment. In the application of wood shakes, interlayment is an 18-inch-wide strip of at least No. 30 felt shingled between each course of shakes so that no felt is exposed to the weather.

jalousie. A window, blind, or shutter with adjustable horizontal slats. A jalousie window has overlapping glass slats that open to allow the passage of air and light.

labeled. Equipment, materials, or products bearing a label, seal, symbol or other identifying mark of a nationally recognized testing laboratory, inspection agency, or other organization whose labeling indicates either that the equipment, material, or product meets identified standards or that it has been tested and found suitable for a specified purpose.

listed. Equipment, materials, products, or services included in a list published by an approved organization that states either that the equipment, material, product, or service meets identified standards or that it has been tested and found suitable for a specified purpose.

live load. Variable loads produced by the use and occupancy of the building, such as people and furnishings, not including construction or environmental loads produced by dead loads or by wind, snow, rain, earthquake, flood, or dead loads.

local exhaust. An exhaust system that uses one or more fans to exhaust air from a specific room or rooms (typically bathrooms and kitchens) within a dwelling.

luminaire. Complete lighting unit (lighting fixture) consisting of a lamp or lamps, together with parts designed to distribute the light, to position and protect the lamps and ballast, and to connect the lamps to the power supply.

makeup air. Air that replaces the air being exhausted from a room or structure.

means of egress. A continuous and unobstructed vertical and horizontal path from any occupied portion of a dwelling to the exterior of the dwelling at the required egress door, without requiring travel through a garage.

O.C. On-center spacing of studs, joists, rafters, or fasteners.

on-site non-potable water reuse systems. Water systems for the collection, treatment, storage, distribution, and reuse of non-potable water generated on site, including but not limited to graywater systems. This definition does not include rainwater harvesting systems.

overcurrent protection device. A circuit breaker, fuse, or other device that protects the circuit by opening the device, thereby disconnecting power to the circuit, when the current reaches a value that causes excessive heat in conductors (overcurrent).

performance. Design and construction to ensure the building system will function in a certain way to meet the building code's minimum requirements. Performance to meet structural requirements is typically achieved through engineering.

prescriptive. When referring to code provisions, a specific set of rules the builder may follow to assure code compliance.

psf. Pounds per square foot.

PVC. Polyvinyl chloride.

R-value. A measure of resistance to heat flow through a given thickness of material, typically insulation. A higher R-value means a greater thermal resistance.

rabbeted. With a recess or groove cut into the edge, as in a piece of wood.

racking. Movement of structural elements out of level or plumb by the lateral forces of wind, earthquake ground motion, or other loads.

ready access (to) (readily accessible). That which enables a device, appliance or equipment to be directly reached, without requiring the removal or movement of any panel, door or similar obstruction.

safe room. A storm shelter.

seismic. Characteristic of or having to do with earthquake ground motion.

seismic design category (SDC). A classification assigned to a structure based on its occupancy category and the severity of the design earthquake ground motion at the site.

solar heat gain coefficient (SHGC). The ratio of the solar heat gain entering the space through a window assembly to the incident solar radiation. The lower a window's solar heat gain coefficient, the less solar heat it transmits.

stack vent. Continuation of the waste stack above the highest horizontal drain connection.

structural composite lumber. Structural members manufactured using wood elements bonded together with exterior adhesives.

structural insulated panel (SIP). A panel that consists of a lightweight foam plastic core securely laminated between two thin, rigid wood structural panel facings.

toilet room. A room containing a water closet and, frequently, a lavatory, but not a bathtub, shower, spa, or similar bathing fixture.

townhome (townhouse). A building that contains three or more attached townhome units.

townhome (townhouse) unit. A single-family dwelling unit in a townhome that extends from foundation to roof and that has a yard or public way on not less than two sides.

trap primer. A device that automatically replenishes water in a trap to maintain the trap seal. Trap primers typically serve floor drains that may lose their trap seal through evaporation because of infrequent use.

U-factor. The rate of heat loss through a window or door assembly. The lower the U-factor, the greater the resistance to heat flow.

ungrounded conductor. Generally referred to as the "hot" conductor (wire). The insulation color is typically black or red, but may be of any color other than white, green, or gray.

vapor diffusion port. An assembly constructed or installed within a roof assembly at an opening in the roof deck to convey water vapor from an unvented attic to the outside atmosphere.

waste receptor. A floor sink, standpipe, hub drain or a floor drain that receives the discharge of one or more indirect waste pipes.

waste stack. A main line of vertical DWV piping that conveys only liquid sewage not containing fecal material.

whole-house mechanical ventilation system. An exhaust system, supply system, or combination thereof, designed to mechanically exchange indoor air for outdoor air when operating continuously or through a programmed intermittent schedule to satisfy the whole-house ventilation rate.

windborne debris region. Areas within hurricane-prone regions located in accordance with one of the following:

- Within 1 mile of the coastal mean high water line where the ultimate design wind speed, V_{ult}, is 130 mph or greater.
- In areas where the ultimate design wind speed, V_{ult}, is 140 mph or greater; or Hawaii.

wood structural panel. A panel manufactured from veneers or wood strands or wafers bonded together with waterproof synthetic resins or other suitable bonding systems. Examples of wood structural panels are plywood, OSB, or composite panels.

wye fitting. Also referred to as a Y-fitting. A plumbing fitting with a Y shape, usually with one arm at a 45° angle to the main fitting.

Index

access
  attics, 200
  crawl spaces, 81
  mechanical systems, 230–231
additions, alterations, and repairs
  carbon monoxide alarms, 53–54
  engineered wood products, 94, 194
  smoke alarms, 31
  trusses, 96
AFCI (arc-fault circuit interrupters), 328–329
air admittance valves, 287–288
air conditioning. *See* mechanical systems
air gaps, 270–271
air infiltration, 55
air intake openings, 55, 208
air leakage, 223–224
air-impermeable insulation, 198–199
alarms, 30–31, 53–54
alterations. *See* additions, alterations, and repairs
appliances. *See also* fuel gas
  in attics, 231, 243–244